Honoring Nature

Published by Human Error Publishing
Paul Richmond
www.humanerrorpublishing.com
paul@humanerrorpublishing.com

Copyright © 2021
by
Human Error Publishing & NatureCulture

All Rights Reserved

ISBN: 978-1-948521-49-9

Front Cover:
Photosynthesis by Martin Bridge https://www.thebridgebrothers.com

Back Cover
NatureCulture
&
Human Error Publishing

Human Error Publishing asks that no part of this publication be reproduced or transmitted in any form or by any means electronic or mechanical, including photocopy, recording or information storage or retrieval system without permission in writing from Human Error Publishing and NatureCulture. The reasons for this are to help support the publisher and the artists.

Individual copyrights stay with the authors and with the artists.

Honoring Nature

An Anthology of Authors and Artists
Festival Writers

Edited by Lis McLoughlin, PhD

Published by
Human Error Publishing
Wendell, MA

Welcome to the Woods

-We are part of Nature.

-We need to interact with the natural world as living kin, not dead resource.

-We can do it.

These are the messages that thread their way through the writings in this volume. Each essay, each poem, each image asserts these truths either in so many words, or as an example of how to live them.

When I first brought together this diverse group of writers for the Authors and Artists Festival (2020-2021), most had one thing in common---I (or Paul Richmond, who curated many of the poets) knew them from somewhere. That somewhere could have been through their pages decades ago, or a serendipitous meeting that blossomed into friendship just recently. I felt grateful to have each one in my life, and that could have been enough.

But once amalgamated, I found in these writings something more. Together, they are no less than a coalition, a coalescence of life's purpose. Too close to my own work to see these connections, it took the synergy of these 37 writers---their passion, their clarity, their truth--to highlight the path we have been walking, individually and in collaboration. Not lost in a laurel hell (although sometimes it feels that way), nor retracing a blue-blazed trail maintained for easy passage of many feet; ours is more of a deer path, the most intuitive and unobtrusive way up the side of a hill. For me, reading these words is like hearing echoes from deer that have trod this way before, and they keep me going when the way seems long and steep.

As winter draws in, under hemlock, in these pages, we've yarded up together, and we know---I know--we are not alone. As Scott Russell Sanders has written, "There's only one league--and all who love reading and writing and nature belong to it."

There is room for you too. Join us in Honoring Nature.....

10/30/20
L. McLoughlin
Hemlock House, Northfield, MA

Table of Contents

I. Listening to Nature

Practiced Invisibility - Marty Espinola	12
13 lines tied to the wind - Janet MacFadyen	13
Bear Swamp Sequence - Janet MacFadyen	14
Pierpont Meadow - Robert Eugene Perry	16
Breaking Silence - Candace Curran	17

Plants

Lines written upon a blank leaf - Roger West	20
Red - Cheryl Savageau	21
Scrub Oak, Pitch Pine - Janet MacFadyen	22
Writing Santa Clara Valley - Susan Glass	23
Waiting for Lilacs - Dina Stander	24
Hawksbeards or maybe Cats Ears but not Dandelions - Kate Rex	25
Butterflies 1 - Kate Rex	26
Brexit - Kate Rex	27

Rivers

Susurration - Robert Eugene Perry	30
Conjunction (Perryville Dam) - Robert Eugene Perry	31
Besides the River - Carlos Raúl Dufflar	32
Swift River-Kancamagus - Cheryl Savageau	33
The Salmon Go All the Way Upstream - Anna M. Warrock	35

Sky

Untitled - Cindy Snow	38
Anchor in the sky - Janice Sorensen	39
Geese on the Wing - Marty Espinola	41

II. Identity

Wild Onions - JuPong Lin	44
Under Cedar Boughs - JuPong Lin	45
Canvas - Holly Harden	46
Birds in Winter - Candace Curran	47
Oh, it can be good to forget. - Janice Sorensen	48
Moving on After That Rotten Announcement - Janice Sorensen	50
The Monastery - Paul Rabinowitz	51
Soundscape - Paul Rabinowitz	52

III. Human-Animal Relationships

Adaptation - Cindy Snow	56
Monarchs - David Crews	57
A Small Healing - Susan Glass	63
The Cat - Paul Rabinowitz	65

IV. Warnings and Destruction

Thin Bears - Jason Grundstrom-Whitney	70
Yes We Have No Bananas - Candace Curran	72
LEVIATHAN - Richard Wayne Horton	73
Cetus Fornax - Roger West	76
Lepidoptera helicoptera - Roger West	80
Hiroshima Shadow - Karen Warinsky	81
oxygen producers - Zarnab Tufail	82
The Tower (Upright) - David Wyman	83
2020 Hindsight - d.o.	84

V. Finding Hope

Clouds, Hopes, Dreams - Paul Richmond	92
Puerto Rican Garden Dream - Ángel L. Martínez	94
johnny-jack - Dina Stander	95
When We Can Breathe - JuPong Lin	96
Rock Bowl - Jason Grundstrom-Whitney	97

VI. Stories of Art, Science, and Adventure

Blow - Lise Weil	102
Oceans of Love - G.A. Bradshaw	105
The Ember - Rebecca R Burrill	113
Mountain Meditation -Leo Hwang	117
Tree of Souls - Joan Maloof	119
The Voices Return - Christian McEwen	121
Every River Wants to Flow - Susan Cerulean	123
Finding Hope in a Web of Mutuality - Deb Habib	127

VII. Stories of Faith

What is it for - Cheryl Savageau	132
Walking the Land of the Nailbourne - Simon Wilson	134
The Whole Inexpressible Thing - Julia Sibley-Jones	136

Afterword

The Enchantment of Nature and the Nature of Enchantment   142
Patrick Curry

Postscript   148
Doug Harris

Authors' Biographies   150

Credit for Previous Publication   156

Artists' Credits   157

Acknowledgements   159

I. Listening to Nature

Great White Egret Fishing by Marty Espinola

Practiced Invisibility
Marty Espinola

Being still,
Standing statuesque
In water and mud
Above fish and frog,
It seeks to appear as one
With the sky shapes above.

A furtive, frozen form
Merging itself
With light and shadow
Waiting for a wavering prey
That, seeing the expected,
Senses only safety.

When the prize is offered
A swift blurred strike
An upward thrust of the head
As the Egret proudly swallows
And calmly resumes
Practiced invisibility.

13 lines tied to the wind
Janet MacFadyen

the red squirrel runs right towards us then straight up a tree
how surprised he is   how strange
to stand in the middle of a wood not knowing what we are

the wind will not stop blowing
it is not put off by the jibber of news   it is not tied to a profit
    it is simply unspooling
I could mimic it   be birdsong or the red hurricane of fur
when I say wind I really mean voices   I really mean the yellow death
    caps rising out of leafmeal
I'm asking you to listen
I'm asking to see how the leaves underfoot lay down their bodies as a
    sentence
I try to read but I understand only what I already know

following lines of broken sticks   abandoned nests   the wind
    tells us to keep moving
set intention aside   do what we have to do
    birds also singing
in the last fused hours of daylight

Bear Swamp Sequence
Janet MacFadyen

A diamond of sun
rips across the surface
of a ruffling pond—
wide blade of a spear
aimed directly at me.

～～

They must
love each other to be
so entwined, two trees
whose roots
embrace, muscular
as pythons.

Straight trunk with a seam
stitched up its side, and
fused to its root the stub
of a hollowed-out stump
—brother long dead, the scar
still alive.

～～

Cut copper birch
sprouts a dozen
small shoots
rooted in rock
on the side
of an outcrop,
stubborn as anything
that walks this earth.

～～

Words emerge
in drifts of gold.
We feel them

through booted soles,
swirls that speak
to toe prints, leaves
freely flung
as a text to read.

~~

Gold beech
Yellow birch
A pond mirroring
A mackerel sky
That mirrors
The disk of water
The life of fish
The mind
Turns inward
The voice
Turns inward
I am here
Not there
This is how it is

~~

I scrunched through leaf fall
to a sheer cliff face
of peeling lichen, intaglio
of root and branch
overlooking a cleft
running down to the bowl
of a marsh.   A chipmunk
was as noisy as I, a gray squirrel
also—nothing could move
without first announcing itself.
I heard footsteps of something—
upsweep of energy, wind
coming in—leaves giving voice
in a single breath.

Pierpont Meadow

Robert Eugene Perry

bare feet on the grassy path
spring births unparalleled joy
this conduit between worlds
grass gives way to rough needles

tall pines arch
a portal to silence, introspection
whispers weaving through the forest
evergreen slicing my dull senses awake

a stream bends through
marsh grass and cattails
sliding under the path
to the waiting pond

now the trail forks, to the right
a wooded path will reach the water
to the left will loop
past the sunning beaver's dam

cycles, seasons, changes –

the gestation of spring,
dance of summer rhythms,
circles of fall, all lie down
and sleep in winter.

Breaking Silence
Candace Curran

A lone diving duck
early morning reflections
popping clouds

A puppeteered prop
self correcting as she goes
at a loss for words

Constant questioning
mantra of a bluetick hound
this neck of the woods

All of us with masks
not everyone is smiling
eye of the racoon

Bullseye of deer
inciting target practice
under full Buck Moon

From the viper's tongue
crooked river chemistry
she makes the call

Listening to Nature: Plants

Embracing the Light by Vic Berardi

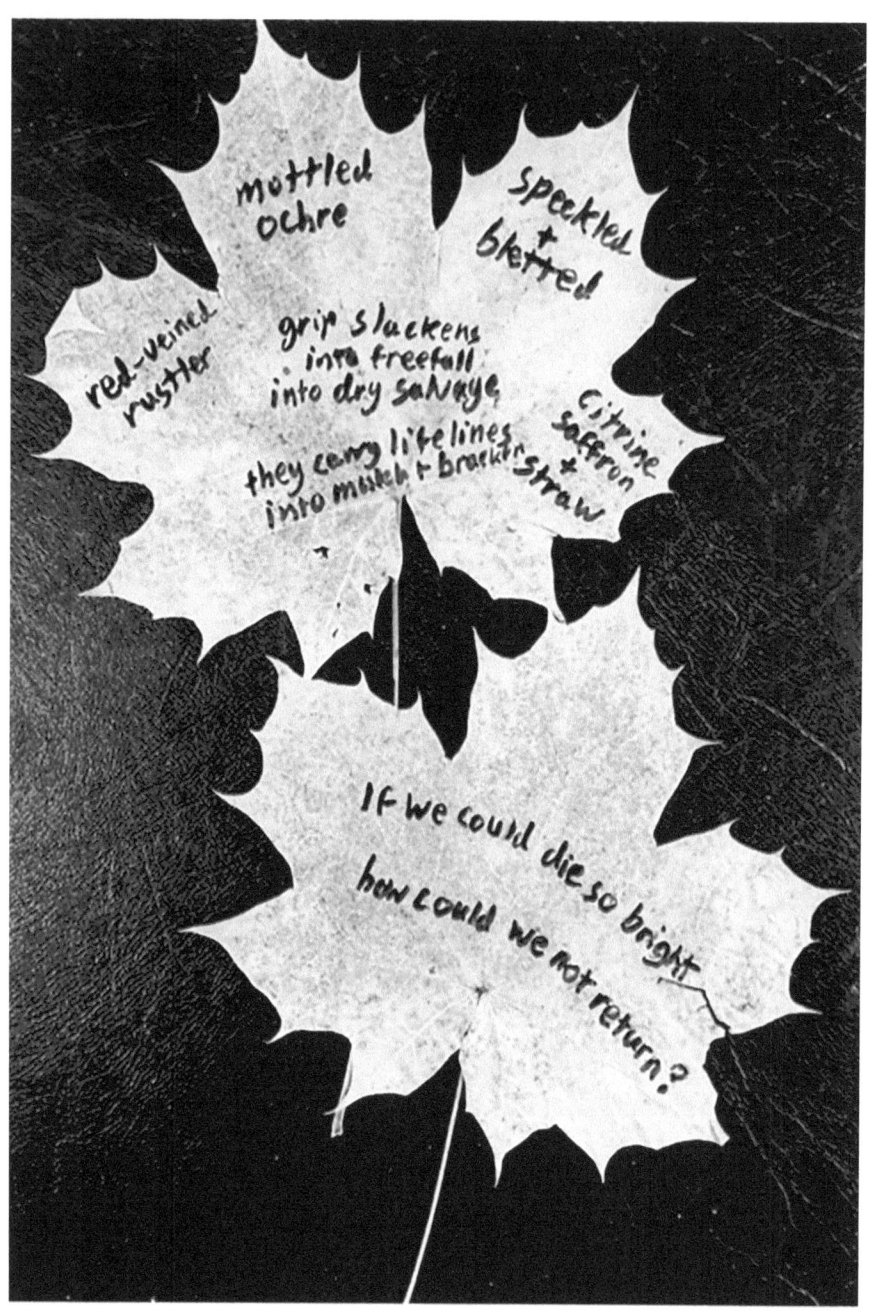

Lines written upon a blank leaf
Roger West

Red
Cheryl Savageau

In his new poem
the red autumn woods
are a metaphor
for leftist martyrs
We are traveling east through a maple forest
that blazes the hillsides on both sides of this winding
back-country road Look at the trees I want to tell him
Listen The trees have their own stories to tell
like the story of fire deep within the heart They too
have been martrys in the long war against the land, a nation
cut down, children denied
A hundred years ago these hills were bare of trees
the stone walls that wind through them
the illusion of ownership Now the hills are red with maples
My heart is leaping out to meet them, my eyes
cannot be full enough Though acid falls from the clouds
maples have gathered on the hillsides
in every direction See how they celebrate
They are wearing their brightest dresses
Come sisters, let me dance with you
I offer you a song
Let me paint
it red with
passion
You are
all the women
I have ever loved

....*for Chrystos*

Scrub Oak, Pitch Pine
Janet MacFadyen

Let me be
so alive as these
desiccated leaves
moving all their lives
from mold to salt,
wind to wind.
And look! a pitch
pine's boa-
constrictored limbs
drape over us,
wrap around what-
ever they claim—air
and its blueness, ar-
thritic-fingered oaks, all
unnoticed until
we sit on this
split rail fence
greyed out from
salt and moisture.
We are of
this world, fashioned
of salt and breath.
May we be
as patient as this
old one next to
me, whose lower
branches grip
its spent bleached
cones, be-
wreathed with lichen
—also grey—a smoky
pitch pine, grey-
thumbed, grey-eared
listening
with quiet
memory.

Writing Santa Clara Valley
Susan Glass

I wish my words were acorns,
my lines, stems and branches
my tap root, this whole line of brown foothills.
I hope for poems made
from sycamore leaves whose edges curl a warning in drought.
I want corrugated stanzas
I can scratch my back against,
stanzas too wide to reach my arms around.
I need lyrics that don't fear
coyote scat, or a great horned owl's silent wing.
I believe in scrub jay voices raking the undergrowth,
and in the assonance
of autumn water falling.
I yearn for poems whose downed limbs bruise
my shins as I leap across streams
and sting my nose with tar weed scent.
It is never enough to write or say or remember:
"quail."
A poem must be the line of fledglings
stepping single file along the rancher's fence,
or pip, pip, pippping
in the chaparral.

Waiting for Lilacs
Dina Stander

that fleeting season
of showers and flowers
anxiety over a late frost
peepers
salamanders
robins and bees
a phoebe building a nest above the front door again
(persisting although this never goes well)
turtle crossings
the rhubarb erupts
garlic is up
then peas
herbs wintered over
thyme sage lemon-balm
the marjoram too
dandelions
crocus
daffodils
tulips
the coltsfoot comes and goes
the trillium bows in
the bluets tremble
even the magnolia that's grown huge is just an opening act
we are all waiting in anticipation of that one deep breath
checking out the window each morning
will this be the day (the glorious day!)
for the last of the cold in our bones to let go
will this be the day the lilacs bloom?

Hawksbeards or maybe Cats Ears but not Dandelions
Kate Rex

When we opened our front door they were there, waiting for us
bunched together, in a straggly line,
joyfully irregular, leaning over, criss-crossing each other.
Making a different sense of the boundary between the big flat stones
and the dusty chips behind.

There was almost a trembling,
anticipation of our pleasure in their presence.
No more than a centimetre in diameter, each head was made of 50 or more flowers, packed in, standing petal, to petal building that intensity of yellow absorbed from somewhere else to be reflected back just for us.

It was their morning of absolute perfection.
We carried it with us through the day.

I opened the door to say goodnight.
They were one step ahead of me
closed shut, protected until morning.

Butterflies 1
Kate Rex

Butterflies the colour of other plants land on the tips of pale blue
flowers that struggle to maintain some balance in the wind
They land untidily,
and hang off one petal.
Using all their legs they clamber up into the cup with not the slightest
respect for the fragile parts they use to give them leverage.

They introduce a disequilibrium that cannot be righted even after
they've gone.
They are the wrong tone, they're the wrong everything
Their colour next to the pale blue excites no vibration.

There is however some exchange in the centre that benefits both.

Brexit
Kate Rex

Listening to Nature: Rivers

Enders Falls by Marty Espinola

Susurration
Robert Eugene Perry

(in) a language all its own, the river
speaks in susurrus, syllables
sometimes sibilant, soft
slaps of waves over stones,
sweeping sensuously across branches,
swirling into eddies around corners,
speaking in soothing textures,
showing off its splendor –
singing surreptitiously
        for those with ears to hear.

Conjunction (Perryville Dam)
Robert Eugene Perry

This is the sweet spot
where time slows.

The marsh explodes with sound
red wings caw
full throated joy
calling to make life –

a wood drake observes
from the channel
patiently awaiting
his chance to impress.

Slowly moving water
heading for cataracts
               just downriver

patchwork of greens and browns
new growth sprouts from decay

the river flowing over the dam
background music for the bog
bright red buds on trees
highlighted by overcast skies.

Standing on the bones of my ancestors

I am here, now.

Besides the River
Carlos Raúl Dufflar

Open my soul beneath the trees along the Cooper River and enters
into the Delaware
The sunshine is such a beauty
That lays upon the heart
The season of autumn
While the leaves turn orange
Branches of the living sky
The geese are enjoying dinner all over the grass
On the small space on the land
In the Land of the Lenape
It's a good moment to see the sunset
squash, cranberries, blueberries or pumpkin
So close to the eyes
Precious space on Mother Earth
That we must honor and respect
No deniers of the beauty of Earth and its love
Laughing that opens his mouth like an empty soul
Sunday afternoon sitting and remembering
Ralph Featherstone and Che Payne Robinson
Fifty winters ago
That must never be forgotten
Martyrs of the Human Rights Struggle
That are part of you and part of me
Listen to the harmony voices
And the sounds of Miles Davis and A Kind of Blue
A rare gift
I enjoy this moment of this year 2020
That life is worth a thousand poems
In honor of the Earth
While the raven dances a bebop tune
October morning sun
Leaves a ripening to Fall
The Indigenous call to honor Mother Earth

Swift River - Kancamagus
Cheryl Savageau
        ...for Lisa

we pull off the road
to this place
where in summer
swimmers
loll on the rocks
like otters
grandmothers
and grandbabies
wade in the icy
shallows where
sand has been pounded
soft and teenagers
dive into deeper
pools and come
out shining
beaded with water

today it is just us
and we walk out
over the boulders
find one mid-river
and sit, back to back

we have just driven
down the Kancamagus
from the high spot
that separates
the watersheds
one flowing east,
the other west and south
the directions of her
people and mine

We laugh to realize
she is facing west
I am facing east

we've done this without
thinking
someday someone will
find two women in rock
back to back
on this mountain
facing sunset, facing dawn

The Salmon Go All the Way Upstream
Anna M. Warrock

The fish gather in the cold ocean,
breathe water, eat other fish.
They in turn are eaten. What do they know?
They know they are salmon and where
they were born. They gather in the cold ocean,
and when it is their turn to die,
when it is their turn to return, they know
what to do. They remember where
they need to go, and they go. The female salmon
stop roaming the ocean, eating other fish.
They leave the endless deep and turn
toward land to find the river mouth
that spit them forth. They enter the mouth,
go upriver. The female salmon travel together.
The male salmon leave the cold ocean,
the eating of other fish. They seek
the mouth that spit them forth
from the land's constriction, and enter.
They go back guided by the memory.
They go to make the memory
continue in their way. They go to make
the salmon continue in the old way.
They swim upriver, leap the falls,
push between rocks, against water
to the shallows where they were born.
They go to the heart of the land. They meet
and agree. The female waves her body
and lays her eggs and moves off. The male
waves his body, sprays his seeds and moves off.
Then the female and male salmon die.
In the shallows, having given birth
to eggs and seeds, a promise to their memories,
they die. The salmon go all the way upstream.
The salmon go all the way to death.

Listening to Nature: Sky

Desert View Watchtower by Cate Woolner

Untitled
Cindy Snow

The night's thin
blue-purple cape
is rimmed crimson,
now orange fire,
now honey yellow.

Here's the sun.
Here's morning.

Anchor in the sky
Janice Sorensen

    your round face
    it is not fair

                                                 my sleepless listing
                                               it is   it is not   is it   is it

    your solid directions
               through the cloudy world
                                            warm attentive night

    tearing parchment
    shining down

                                              making me split

                                            fragilethin

    You the path
    brightrighteoushope

                               your beacon crosshairs
                               +expose+and+confuse+me+

    cool tug and tide
    the crucifying synapsis

                        to find myself ← I escape →
                        you

not like me at all

                            hold steady

anchor in the night sky

                                                you do not
                                                wait for me

to
                remember
to
                swim
to
                shore

                              a fish caught in the hull
too awake too sleep
                              too hungry too eat
      too, too much air

                              to breathe and finally,

I float

                            absorbent

                                              and
                          murky

                s w e l l I n g I n t h e b I l g e

Geese On the Wing
Marty Espinola

Arrows of wild geese,
Autumn driven towards a perpetual horizon,
Endlessly waving their wings to the god of winds.
Do they just trust their leader knows the way?
Or is their trust in the pull of the beyond,
Knowing that moving towards it is enough?
It makes me wonder.
Is the direction all that's really important?

II. Identity

Canoe Catch by JuPong Lin

Wild Onions
JuPong Lin

Out beyond ideas of wrongdoing and rightdoing
there is a field...I'll meet you there.
                    --Rumi

Greeting the sun, we touch the screens
on our phones to locate our bodies,
check pockets for don't-leave-home-without-it devices,
eyes enthralled by machines that conjure faces, other places,
others' homes.
In the twittering, 24-7 texting,
networked clouds of virtual connection,
where do we hit pause?
When do we ask…
Who may suffer for our pleasure?
Who sweats black tears to craft
our treasures? Whose lives are made
more beautiful by technological wonders?
Out beyond the zeros and ones,
there is a real
field. Meet me there, and we will fill
our pockets with acorns and rocks
and stories, listen to night critters and ache
for the fragrance of wild ginger and
onion flowers.

Under Cedar Boughs
JuPong Lin

For Chi

Tomorrow, we should walk in the rain,
he says. Birds sound sweeter
and cedar smells more pungent.
Soft drips fill the spaces
of our slowly spoken thoughts.

We name ferns—deer and sword,
licorice and lady.
My belly wells up with regret
for pulling up the roots he set down
in these old forests.

Tomorrow a plane whisks my body
into the other life,
where neither of us ever felt at home.

"My place," the one his brother
calls home every other week, is where
we know which cabinet corner
stashes the chocolate, which window
Is best for glimpsing the squirrels nabbing sunflower.
Home hides behind a fog
of unrealized dreams and mistaken loves.
Tomorrow I'll make shelter for your dreams,
my two boys. I will make up for lost
time, and together we will learn
to say "rain" in many tongues,
in renga, scat and in my
mother's tongue, Hokkien.

Canvas
Holly Harden

I am alive, but not near enough.
I gather wood through the days and
In the nights these same ragged hands reach to the sky
Like small hummingbirds for sugar, for red.
I want to be the canvas of the hammock
Between the oaks,
Near a garden someone planted first in a dream.
The canvas of a painting
Someone thought about painting
Walking in twilight hours along an old dirt road.
The canvas of a coat I wear when there's frost on the ground
And my breath makes small clouds that fade into the air
And reappear later, near the fire, in my tired eyes.
The canvas of the tent staked in a field where there is nothing
But the scent of wheat grass and earth, and the sky
Over that rise where the deer gather
At the edge of the forest.
You know that dream, where you wait and always will wait
For someone to come walking over that hill,
Carrying a pail of berries, perhaps,
Or an axe, cheeks blushed from the sun and wind.

Perhaps that is what we are, each of us.
A canvas for the earth.
That thought returns like a tide, like a moon,
like morning fog on the lake.
These hands are rivered and bramble-scarred.
I hear an owl calling.
Cover me with leaves.

Birds in Winter
Candace Curran

Falling branch to branch
An avalanche of blue jays
Toss icy snowballs

and everyone makes a run for it   grey squirrels in starts and stops the cannonball sun rolling out of town   making her want to ski-pole stab snowbanks   to detonate and undo herself   try to kill time or make peace with half past four   and giving in to giving up going home where happiness has unraveled somehow   won't stay won't sit at the kitchen table and think things through   hash things out   leaving her all by herself to restuff and restring Scarecrow to pick over the jumble of his cryptic bones   to insert herself again inside the hideyholes of his fractured corset   a temporary sanctuary for a bird like her a   safehouse until it isn't

His shirts on the line
Ghostlighting in the half-light
Frozen prayer flags

Oh, it can be good to forget.
Janice Sorensen

Once you were a secret, warm and forming
golden goo, next, chipping pecking pushing
with crazy might to emerge.
Now, a chicken, you
      hide
      cluck
      struggle to get your egg out.

Or, a tadpole (once an egg too!)
now morphed peeping desperate
swimming toward life
in the balance, immediate
in the instinct-driven state
of ignorant vigilance,
      soon to rest in perfect peace
        in the belly of perfect peace.

Or, as the caterpillar,
weaving into the struggle
of the sweet fat crystalline
hungry snuggle toward bliss
when jellied oooo becomes
wet parchment and splint. Toward the day
when a cross breeze has more meaning
than the long earthy journey.

Or even when you are no longer
a tapered icicle but slipply dripping mixed
to mud soon heaved as morning frost; then
      to vapor—

but but that is not the end.

Not until you are pulled
to your bubbled and boiling potential—
not until the lick of the flames lets go of the dance
or, you rise from the heat of this glowing coil

will you wonder if you are remembering something,
following orders
      or making this up as you go?

Moving on After That Rotten Announcement
Janice Sorensen

                      I feel it happening:

the sea lions are yelling

the air is overly moist

and an elk has lost it's way

a seal is jerky dry and bloated

on the coastal beach rocks

where a gull awaits patiently

            (for what
            I can only guess)

perhaps for my belly to burst
            with the rotten
            ANNOUNCEMENT
                          that I have

                              fallen

                        out of favor

                      with the world.

The Monastery
Paul Rabinowitz

Unable to finish
my latest poem
I return to the
buddhist monastery

The meditation garden
In full bloom,
lilac and mint

My teacher says
to observe the natural order
draw her from memory,
shadows and lines,
symmetry, proportion

Then without touching
my bald head,
or wrinkled face,
explore the broken parts,
draw a self portrait,
through her eyes

Compare, be ready
to choose

Return and finish
the poem
or stay, observe,
autumn colors,
mist after rain,
death in winter

Soundscape
Paul Rabinowitz

After making coffee
much the same way
every morning
I cover my head
with a favorite hoodie
click on ocean wave
soundscape
and prepare
for the act
of another little poem
about the way
I feel about you
but nothing

                except   metaphors

  seagulls   distant shores

and recall
the first time
Tom Waits
spinning
on your player
something about
Ahab and drifting

III. Human-Animal Relationships

Untitled by Fred Bulye

Adaptation
Cindy Snow

She wants to crawl
like a newt   a little hip   a little warning.   Every
rock just a rock.   Every twig, no longer living
and hurtful.

A newt carries
its Bo Diddley beat across damp leaf litter.   Forget
camouflage.   She's brilliant orange   yellow spotted.

Rotting cherries scattered   red/black.   The newt navigates.
Robins
poke the dirt by her toe.   The newt soldiers on.
A harvest wasp
lands on her leg.   The newt freezes.   The wasp flies off.

It's a rare thing   a newt   persistent.

She holds it
in her hand, feels its heart
against its belly, and
think, think, thinks
of something   other than plunder.

Monarchs
David Crews

The leaves are turning

in the valley it is difficult to notice

        but once atop bedrock

open sky preserves color

What do you see?

It's like they are floating
                she says

There are so many

drifting to endless blue

        Where are they going?

They follow currents south

to breed

At one point monarch meant

        supreme governor of life—

the fifty daughters of Danaus

King of Argos

who killed their husbands

        on wedding nights

condemned to underworld

>   to draw water

in bottomless buckets

futile labor—
>   *Danaus plexippus*

>   I wish we could see it

this sleepy transformation

the Greeks name—
>   hibernation, metamorphosis

The kingdom *Animalia* includes animals

then invertebrates—

>   having not
and still becoming

caterpillar, chrysalis
>   butterfly

that we name
>   *Arthropoda*, insect

What is it

striking or jumping or floating

along the ridge?

I feel each one pulled

by a string, and it makes me

>   a child again

The glaciers of the last ice age

instigated migration—

some go to deserts in the west

some mix
          with sedentary populations

in the tropics—Central America

              the Caribbean

travelers
          solo natives

and they are different

          in behavior and shape

Some fly

over eleven hours straight

without feeding
          four thousand miles

to Sierra Madre de Oriente

the Gulf of Mexico

It is a marvel they know where to go

          I will remember this day

of cairns, sky
          and monarchs

Do you remember

when we first came here

                monarchs by the thousands

Now, neighbors plant milkweed—

scarlet milkweed, pinewood

                milkweed, swamp

and butterfly
              milkweed

Its pattern, they say, repels

predatory birds

      but their diet

makes them toxic
              Still

they are in trouble?

What if they could see what we see

here, right now

maybe others would save trees

      plant milkweed

and remember these creatures

as a wonderous flight of the living

Then

they might always have a place

     to go

Do you remember
     that day

on the ridge trail to the summit

the sky so blue, and those wisps

of cloud
    and monarchs

drifting in wind?

The image of them
      remains

so vivid, so earthly and ours

     I want to say

I love you
     and love too

there are moments we have shared

moments inside this world

we call
  life, the living

    the self-willed land

what is easily forgotten when gone

Maybe one day

you might paint this memory

how you love

to make the world
 feel alive

and beautiful

*after Cathy Hartung's painting
(NorthWind Fine Arts, Saranac Lake, NY, April 2020)*

A Small Healing
Susan Glass

Ada's spine is a notched cane where recurring pains
deliver stings: pinched nerves to the brain.
The postures of onset blindness,
looking always down at first, and then always up,
toward daylight, toward voices,
have sculpted her carriage.
So too the loss of name to marriage.
Oh to breathe! To be March grass, Mustard scent!
She rises in the clear dawn,
and walks.

Horses wait for her,
nestled in the curve of a half suburban road.
She smells them first:
their molasses breath, their wool musk coats, now winter-shed.
Appaloosa, Roan, Palomino, Bay.
She approaches. Their skins wriggle,
and their ears, gliding forward to catch her steps,
are wreathed in dew.

For much of this past night, they have stayed awake,
quickened by apricot blossoms and frog chorus.
She imagines their conversation,
stories of space before fence and bridle,
before myth even —
Thinks, too, of their sleepwalker dreams,
amblings, alder lust,
envies them,
regrets career and mortgage,
the swaddling walls that hold her life.

The Morgan Bay approaches first.
She's a filly still, and Ada,
hearing the bamboo jointed shamble of long-boned knees,
feels again the gentlest pressure
of thigh against flank.

A demure head stretches over braided wire,
bobs the long nose, pole, forelock.
Invites a scratch.
Ada obliges,

offers carrots too as the others sidle close,
buzz their lips,
swat each other with broom straw tails.

On tiptoe Ada stretches,
loses her face in the feral mane,
inhales the milk-warm, new filly breath,
feels the new girl, clean laundered, and T shirt fresh,
leaping straight-backed and lithe
from saddle to earth.

The Cat
Paul Rabinowitz

A creaking sound from the old wood floor outside my bedroom starts my mind racing as the large maine coon cat leaps from one stair to the platform of the other pushing open the half closed door with his head and I hear the sound of muffled paws landing gently on the persian carpet as he saunters to the far side of the bed where I sleep then finds his spot and sits in silence to check if I am reacting to his presence but my head is busy organizing a new chapter from our last conversation during our meeting to review progress of the outline for my latest book when you said to me maybe I should write this new novel in close first person to lay out for the world my real feelings not based on some story about an artist that can't find her true self so journeys to an unknown place way up north by a wide river with hawks and osprey and is so taken in by it all she regains inspiration and creates this masterwork and you said this feels forced lacking internal conflict you've admired in my work and remind me that this story has never really happened so the best I can hope for is a few moments when you lean over to check the manuscript and a lock of your hair tucked neatly behind your ear falls away slowly like an eagle in free fall swooping down on something moving

and clutches my forearm at the bone carrying me away to a cloudless sky

and together we circle above the house where my maine coon cat waits patiently for my return and I remember you said maybe I should write a novel based on how I feel when I am alone with you and from this unique vantage point with you gripping me I conjure up poetic verse with rich metaphors to express to the world in that cryptic way I have become so good at when no one except for me and maybe you knows who I am referring to then a gust of wind moves around us and you look over your shoulder at me with those sharp eyes focused on every movement of my mouth as I recite a few lines from this new work and you take me higher to gain more depth through a wider angle and I can look down and see everything even a woman sleeping soundly next to a large maine coon cat who has lost most of his natural instincts handed food that comes from a cannery in an old industrial town near a dark polluted river and I prop up the pillow and with blurry eyes look up at the ceiling and in this new chapter I am organizing in my head I watch another lock of your hair fall away from the other ear and brushes my arm like a single feather caressing an ancient spirit and I am so overwhelmed by this new sense of adventure that I shout through the prevailing winds to take me even higher and soar to a point where I can lose all perspective and my mind will reach some sort of bliss and be inspired to write this new story then suddenly without warning the air speed increases a howling gust breaks the silence then I feel your grip tightening and instinctively you glide into another air pocket for safety and I feel a piercing through my skin spreading over my trusting body creeping slowly inside through a half opened door then feel a sudden jolt of some kind of heavy turbulence bursting wide and landing on my groin with excited claws and I reach for your head and feel vibrations from a familiar purr and glance at the clock on the bedside table hoping it reads something like 7:36 but the red digital lines form the numbers 5:11 which is the same time the large maincoon cat wakes me every morning to commiserate that he too has had a long night and is hungry then leaps down positioning himself on the same spot on the persian carpet by the side of my bed meowing as he has done since the first time when he realized that this is all he needs to do when he is hungry so I dangle my hand near his head as a diversion to calm him in some way as I finish organizing the new chapter in my head but he is more playful than usual

and a claw
like a pin
pricks my finger

and feel blood so I lean over looking down at dilated orange pupils beaming at me in the still version of the breaking dawn

IV. Warnings and Destruction

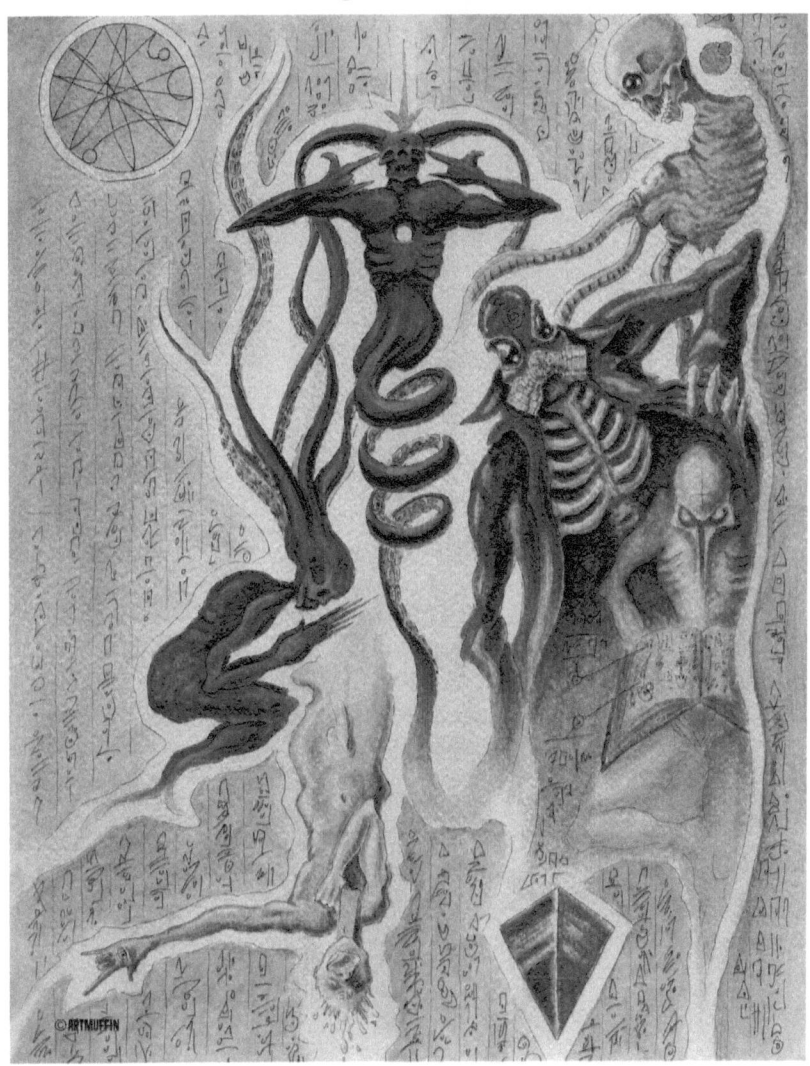

Prophecy Infection by ARTMUFFIN

Thin Bears
Jason Grundstrom-Whitney

Coyote saw an old man
run across a street in Quebec City.
He appeared young, but
on the other side
he stooped again.

"Found another," Coyote said
to Bear at an intersection.

Bear, Raven and Coyote
followed the man
to the back of a packing plant.

In the refrigerator room
they found two women and
the man Coyote had seen on the street.
They were very thin.

"What the hell are you folks doing down here?"
Coyote asked, taking off his hat
and letting the fur flow.

They changed to three thin white bears.

"We come down 35 years ago and
warned the tribes we were dying.
We could see the melt.
Now there is nowhere to hunt.
Countless of us have starved and died,
leaving bones for scrimshaw and medicine.
It is good to leave medicine,
but only in its place and time.
We are moving down."

Bear remembered his sister that died in 2002.
They found her emaciated remains on the edge
of a blueberry field near Calais, Maine.

Coyote and Raven sat with him and prayed
around the sacred fire for four days.

Bear felt death reaching in his new language—
drought, hurricanes, fire, auto-immune illness.
It seemed he added a new word daily.

"Our brothers and sisters warned others,
but the others did not listen."
Bear was angry as he thought of his sister
and the whales he had seen washed onshore
this past summer, their stomachs filled
with plastic.

The thin bears ate slowly so as not to get sick
from the hormone-fed sides of beef.
They stayed for a month until
strong enough to travel.

"There will be many more of us,"
said the old man.

Raven searched for new habitat.
Bear helped them walk.
Coyote encouraged them on.

Each time was getting harder
than the time before.

Yes We Have No Bananas
Candace Curran

In the new trickle down
economy pandemic
Macaque monkeys steal
spray cans   fight turf wars
brawl and reproduce like crazy

they are hungry   starving
they are captured   sedated
castrated and tattooed
released with #'s fast tracking
reproductive rates

since lockdown   since the ban on
travel   tourists with their selfies
trinkets and treats for stealing
no feasts at the temple
no monkey buffet

since the stink of it   unbearable
excrement everywhere
they grow more aggressive
running riot   as uncontrollable
as the virus

the monkeys bury their dead
in the projection room
in the back of an abandoned
cinema in Thai City
where humans live in cages

Scrambling for scraps
we dream ourselves
back into their pockets

LEVIATHAN
Richard Wayne Horton

Stepping out into the suburban whiteness I hold in my hands

these continually passing cars, these lawn sprinklers, these flower beds, these bags of fertilizer, these flushing toilets, these lawn mowers.

Down in the creek fossils washed loose by popular culture have assembled themselves and climbed out to roam the sidewalks carrying an insurance folder

Madam may I speak to the breadwinner?...madam?

Have you ever thought what might happen

if you were to push your hand into the dirt of your back yard and touch the coolness of legacy?

If you were to feel it?

The soil is fatally damp. The leviathan of the land lies below.
He is rock. He cannot be understood

Except by me. I know him. His cold sub-eternal shadow steadies the assassin's sighted gun barrel, so curious to know its prey.

Have you ever walked through submerged cities when you slept,

and heard above you a pounding on the door?

Madam, there are dinosaurs under this town.

Down in the creek children put their feet into dinosaur footprints and pick up pieces of fossilized bone, to duel like crazed reptiles.

The cut away shelf of black clay is a history of Texas murder.

Long winds thunder in their ears. The empty Dallas God speaks without ceasing.

Here we grow, as the suburbs kill us with mildness

Cement floors covered in beige tiles echo the noisy TV, heel bones gettn a beatn when kids walk through in dirty socks. TV commercials, toilet noises, smarmy religious poems painted on picnic plates and tacked to a wall.

The boy's mom makes him go to the store to buy sanitary napkins and ice cream. Later he finds the hidden raunch mags in the garage, hose seams, drug-loosened smiles. Light a cigarette from another cigarette from another cigarette! This is what many men want.

He's out walking when FBI dicks swerve to the roadside. Gov plate on the tail. Join us in the car a sec. Just a string of questions for you today sir. What do you know about certain thugs who've showed up at your house?

The feds, with baloney sandwich breath go through the script a coupla times. What are these interesting individuals' movements? Symphony movements, toilet movements. Trail of evidence leads to catbox.

Interesting. Just real interesting.

Home to the canned corn cackle of TV laughter.

TV goes spawk spawk spawkie…(Blam!) cartoon head gets blown off. "Ya durned varmint!"

The head pops back up and chitters at the fat little hunter who throws his gun on the ground and joins a pacifist cell. Later in a comic strip, a Communist rabbit is discovered and turned in. Comic. Kazi. Commie-crazy.

Saturday he's layin on the bed lookin up at a plastic jet fighter that hangs on a string. The pilot, a spider, bails. He waves a comic book, killing it with humor, then jumps up and hits the road while cows in a field watch.

A motorist stops and asks if he needs to be turned in at a crazy house. "Uh-hhhh, well maybe." Zoom! After a while he tozzles along dizzy, and staggers toward a mirror-topped lake that keeps jumping ahead like propaganda promises. A pickup pulls over. He gets in, and the white haired minister pushes that bible right on over. Big old grin. "That's the answer, son!"

Ballpoint thoughts: suburbs at noon. Dogs gargle near piercing green mimosas. Lawn sprinklers hiss in the womb of whiteness. Kids with sun-bleached hair and brown faces watch from inside a refrigerator box, little blond-haired bugs in the shadows, playing house, holding shadowy teacups.

A newspaper rolls limply across the sidewalk. It has a picture of Jack Ruby, a pointing finger, the back of a head wearing a Stetson. A fierce frown: "Who shot that gun off?"

In back of a church, yellow grass sews across cracks in the black clay. Nearby there's a corrugated iron fence. I can smell the dirt. A face is brown in front of the rusting metal.

In the parking lot

An updraft sends tatters of birds high into the air.

CRASH!..........CRASH!..........

Colossal feet smash into the land, getting closer, bigger than anyone could have thought

I told you! I told you! It's here! He's here! I'm here! There is no past! I am the past!

CETUS FORNAX
Roger West

Hello. This is your tour guide again. As you may have noticed, we have started our descent to this, our final stop of the tour before the evening's seminars, and a chance for you to get out, have a look around and stretch all of your legs.

While you prepare yourselves for arrival, may I have your attention for a short presentation. You should see some images on your screens, the significance of which I will explain in due course.

I know you have been admiring through the cabin windows the lush green vegetation and the clear blue expanses of water that holds an abundance and variety of bird, insect and plant life.

This planet was once inhabited by bipedal hominids known as *Homo habilis*. Yes - a question? That's right, bipedal - just the two legs. I know that seems ridiculously inadequate but they managed like that at first and then when they were no longer content with that, instead of allowing evolution to take its course, they developed individual personal transportations - a development which my colleague Dr Draxon Vulpecular, who will be addressing you later, has pointed out con tributed greatly to what was to come.

Now, *Homo habilis* evolved into *Homo erectus*. Yes, I can hear the laughter going round. *Homo erectus*, yes, and in fact that double entendre that you find so amusing has also been claimed by Professor Velax Quantoris in her new study to be just as much a contributory factor to their downfall.

The next evolutionary stage of these creatures was called *Homo sapiens* - a period which apparently produced a wealth of artistic endeavour, most of which is lost now although the little that remains can be seen in the Museum of the Planets in Pixis Centoris. And *Homo sapiens* of course evolved rapidly into *Homo eroticus*, *Homo bellicose*, *Homo covetous*, *Homo gluttonous* and finally *Homo trumpus*.

Scientific studies into the disappearance of these creatures give us a picture of how the natural world dealt with the threat they posed to it. In their latter stages these creatures produced more and more toxic by-products which they released into their ecosystem. However the ecosystem fought back to prevent its own demise and recycled these toxins back into the hominids through food ingestion, respiratory processes, microbe attacks and - in the case of still-unevolved *Homo erectus* - transmission of bodily fluids. Thus the threat was contained and neutralised and so nature's systematic culling of the species began.

But before we make our preparations for disembarkation, a word of warning. I direct your attention back to the images on your screen - images of the artworks of certain *Homo sapiens* that are on display in the Museum of the Planets. It seems that some of their species did have powers of prophecy and encoded messages in their artworks that warned of the disaster to come. Observe how these hominids are depicted disappearing into the natural world around them - blending, melting, dissolving. And research now points to how their later iterations did exactly that. They did not, as we previously believed, simply die, just vanish from the face of their planet - they became assimilated, subsumed into vegetable and mineral matter. And although they left behind them a planet that looks so beautiful in its pristine purity, the toxicity of its absorbed hominid inhabitants lurks everywhere. So by all means feel free to explore but should you touch, pick up, eat or drink anything, Cetus Fornax Earthtours Inc. will not be held liable for the consequences. That's why we are requiring you to complete and hand in the disclaimer form I am about to distribute before you disembark. Enjoy your visit!

Lepidoptera helicoptera
Roger West

Papillons de nuit. Butterfly/moth: here in France the distinction is temporal rather than entomological. These early morning night butterflies rotorvate putter-puttering around my head. In my path I find a drowsy cicada. I bend down to rescue him from tractor wheels and I'm struck for a moment by his rusty underwings. A woman passing by misconstrues my hesitation. "Elles ne piquent pas," she says - they don't sting - and she scoops the creature up and into the grassy verge. She tells me how her brother used to push a stick into a cicada's anus and throw it into the air to watch it come helicoptering down. "Whereas I," she says, "know that if you turn a cicada over in your hand and gently stroke its stomach, it will sing for you." When she's gone I lift the cicada from its roadside refuge and try to turn it over in my hand. It resists my efforts, clinging desperately to my fingers with all the genetic mistrust it can muster. "I'm not her brother," I tell it. "Neither are you mine," it replies.

Hiroshima Shadow
Karen Warinsky

We will not "repeat the error"
the cenotaph says,
but it seems we only repeat the errors of war
unable to find our way to another path.

Decade upon decade, demand upon demand,
no one backs down, no one finds a new way,
and even the shadow of the man from Hiroshima
blazed into cement steps
is not enough
to move all hearts to peace.

oxygen producers
Zarnab Tufail

ultimately, it comes down to this: we're looking
for shells
under rocks. discharged leftovers
of eukaryotes dead, ages ago. underneath planktons
hustling
food supply
oxygen so we breathe miles away
inside window-less rooms
refuse to take a walk through hills
sit next to the ocean
-swaying producers.

The Tower (Upright)
David Wyman
              to my daughter

Masks appear, panic shoppers clearing
shelves and crashing markets...
(We're afraid of this finality of air.)

Fines are established for breaking the rules.
Here earliest light, a distant gold, sounds like birds.
(We'll see what the world would be without us.)

Parks, trails, entire cities locked up—
entire sports seasons cancelled—
concerts, tours, festivals, events—all cancelled...

Then in the public sphere—the blackening,
this burning away as stubbornly we continue
to live by the old magical notions, even

as satellite images reveal clean industrial skies,
and curious dolphins frolic in Venice canals
and sea turtles invade our deserted beaches.

A momentary vision, dilapidated junk-time.
(In May, armed protestors assaulting the capital.)
OK, well...Be safe, stay in contact

so I don't worry any more than I'm going to
if that's possible. I guess what I'm trying to say,
about this uncertain stumbling, was how

there can be audible silences that cut
the inner ear, and that, taken all together—
It's what we have to harness, to compose...

2020 Hindsight
d.o.

what have we learned from
what we have lived here
land of opportunity lacking
for much unity we
travel in circles victims of
uncertainty or the opposite
often wasting energy, angry
looking for others to blame
driving each other insane
two wings of our one entity
one-hundred years ago we
suffered together so and
soon forgot the pain until
it returned again then bread
lines as far as eyes could
see and the long lost memory
typhoid mary contact tracing
leaders with empathy and
not much attention to the
source of all this pain, sorrow
death and dissolution not to
forget all the confusion.
look over here where the
forests once sheltered so
many creatures now helter
skeltered captured and eaten
sold in cages or tortured and
beaten by humans so
hungry for profit they've
forgotten the comfort of just
living in Nature instead of
their pocket and then get
on guard when we reveal it
or mock it, behavior once scorned
in old tomes and court edicts
now worshipped above all else
another contagion that might not

kill you but could ruin creation
or love and harmony with any given
relation as we witness the end of
countless other lives and existence
of species we are so sadly mistaken
while watching the news, the
plague on our place the chance
of a cure or the latest sensation
which means nothing or worse for
expiring species in diminishing
locations our machines grind down
into "chemical dust" drawn out by
building hot winds into recorded
nightmares of complete devastation.
how much distance have we put
between us and this planet, enough
to make sure whoever's in charge
thinking they ran it were making it
worse through selfish deceit transparent
theatrics folding in stupid with putrid
showmanship apprentice to his own
devolution and posing, always posing
sitting for portraits never hung though
hanging may be too good for some
culling the herd you may have heard
illness self-inflicted and predicted
unspoken requests he please just
get sick and die, we won't cry.
what about those who silent
stood by or bought in with
the sin of hatred exclusion the
ugly fusion muddled illusion
the speeches of mammon more
important than life itself life
once precious as your child
and the wild, the wonder even
the thunder or a sunset or rising
from memory or the moment
where did you just put your
hand in what sequence did

it land near that handle or the
lever and how did the weather
become such a marker outside
that window first lighter then
darker out there where it is
moving about unseen stealth
feeding on everyone's health
just waiting for your reopening
just groping for your lungs and
wagging tongues of freedom
locking and loading and corroding
the steely look in your eyes until
your loved one dies and you follow
suits empty of souls taking endless
tolls on your future your dreams
yelling won't help you be more of
a man reacting to something you
don't understand like the child
you once were still unsure you
react you contract the virus not
guileless and stronger than you.
the price of life what is it how much
the cost of a casket a chair a crutch
is the venting preventing prevention
and such grasping we're asking
for a certain degree of detention
for those we are loath to mention
for their economic pretensions
when time comes unwound day
after day after week when we seek
the usual it goes south to confusional
which moon is it what happened on
what day would you say it is the
worst pandemic in generations or
one hundred years or recorded
history of misery and purposeful
injury original sin and slavery now
kneeling on necks the law on the street
among wrecks burning with anger
short on regrets the monuments

fall and y'all get defensive or is it
ostensive locking and loading
constantly goading as the ground
beneath you slips away what do
you say unmasked in the fray
freedom to get sick and die but
not to drag us along that's wrong
ok?
wrong like that song wrong like
the strong survive about being alive
and all that jive will not survive
imagined blessings no good to crown
no brotherhood in that sound look
around you we surround you we
will take you back but don't react
like some stranger a rearranger of
honesty you are only one third of
the land that you love nothing from
above will change that it's a fact
it's the end of your act time to
go back body politic can't breathe
or breathes too much as such it
is what it is slips from their clutch
an election correction approaches
insurrection may spread the infection
mindless rejection courting hypocrisy
democracy lies with kleptocracy
decency fades amid fascist charades
yet the ballot a mallet bang out some
flaws the avoiding of laws their
sorry lost cause lost again amid plots
amid lots of ugly days turn to weeks
to months our interesting times await
the virus now in the peoples house
finds those who deny and lie who
standby over two hundreds thousands die
but now we elect to make it correct
to deselect to disinfect the body politic
the living planet and those upon it
eject the lunatic with simple arithmetic

counting days of fear to a new year
the end of his reign of pain when it
all felt insane.

V. Finding Hope

The Red Rebel Brigade by Cate Woolner

Clouds, Hopes, Dreams
Paul Richmond

When you open your eyes
What do you see
Are you in a war zone
Are you in the woods
Are you in a hospital ward
Are you seeing death and destruction
Are your seeing beauty
Yoko Ono said living in Japan after the bombings
She only wanted to look up into the sky
To watch the clouds
See how they changed
It gave her hope that things do change
You can dream
You see dragons
Faces
Wild horses
Whole stories unfold
Shown the unfamiliar
The abstract
Formations that don't fit
Into neatly defined boxes
The beauty that is shown and washed away
There is no holding on
Only taking in
Appreciating
Having to let go
The continual changes
The darkness
Then the dawn
The clouds passing over head
Here comes a story
Here comes a storm
Here comes relief from the sun
Look at the beauty
To be overwhelmed
Not to be taken for granted
Will never be the same

It is all there for us to see
Have you looked up
Do you see
Do you feel the hope
Do you dream
Here come the clouds
Here come the clouds

Puerto Rican Garden Dream
Ángel L. Martínez

Can you grow *gandules** in a *barrio* garden
far from home?
(It's still growing)
Did you see a hen and her chicks
on the sidewalk?
(I grew up seeing that in Williamsburg, Brooklyn)
We can grow *los barrios*
Amid the brick-faced crevices

We must never neglect *Madre Tierra*
It's land to plant our flags as well as flowers
A promise made
for *bomba y plena en los jardines*
As son rises from an old radio
And a rooster crows in those spaces liberated
Where we speak our names

*pigeon peas

johnny-jack
Dina Stander

All the hells I don't live in flash across my screen.

Burnt out carcasses of cars and cities, ember-glow skies above the desert, wind driven fires and hounds of war. Women hiding children in their voluminous skirts, veils black as night. I see stars scattered in their creases, burning super novas of maternal power protecting the spark of life and begging mercy from strangers and brothers.

I go searching google images for a remedy to all this, type at random 'hearts ease' and remember the plant that blooms on the page also grows in my garden. Comes up every Spring and stays till snow. 'Hearts Ease' is johnny jump up, a wild viola that plays to our pulses and hides in humble quarters.

Then I go searching the garden to find if any sign of heart's ease will reveal itself on an early June morning that rises too cold. I wander out and bend into mercy, pushing away leaves to find a purple coyote with a winking gold eye tucked in amid the detritus. A johnny-jack trickster that's come wild, surprising me with beauty. A balm for all the ugly hurt humanity hurls.

So I come undone and sit in the garden border between the kitchen herbs and the rhubarb, weeping for all the mothers until my heart finds ease. The crows come then, calling their peace across the day. When I look up and call back (and I swear it's true) I see stars scattered in the black creases of their wings.

When We Can Breathe
JuPong Lin

In the future, my kin morph
into cranes   become, again, ungulates,
urchins   beetle   butterflies   blossoms
magnificent maples sweeping marsh grasses   my name
honors, multitudes mirrored
in my eyes, bursting from dark pupils

In the future we become
other   skin hard as shells, thinning
softening, melting into feathers.
We call each other by name, so many names
in a multitude of tongues   góan tau ě lǎng
mi familia, la famille, chhin-siȯk   親屬, gajok 가족

In the future we are
one   familia, ka-tĕng 家庭 , ohana
not without violence or pain.   Fists raised in
respect strengthens our sinew   if
we can learn to sing, eat, swim, smile together.
In the near future your heart
is my heart. We quiver, we fly, we
breathe   under water and in the sky.

Rock Bowl
Jason Grundstrom-Whitney

Bear carried a drop of
the Atlantic Ocean in a tiny vial.

Raven had flown to the Northwest
and carried back a vial with
a single drop of the Pacific Ocean.

Coyote held a single dewdrop
from a Mountain Ball Cactus flower
from Bryce Canyon.

Three directions—this year it was Deer's turn
for the fourth. She brought a drop of water
from the Colorado River.

They met in northern Arizona,
now called the four corners,
and placed the drops in a rock bowl
they used each year.
Each added sacred medicines—
cedar, sage, sweetgrass,
and tobacco.

They stirred
medicine, water, and fine red earth
into the bowl formation.

Bear prayed over the water
and medicine mixture.
It took longer each year
for this to work.
Water tables ran low;
the ocean cried in pollution.

After several days
the rain fell again.
Bear, Coyote, Raven, and Deer

fell asleep near the rock bowl
and dreamed of golden tassels of corn

singing in the southeastern breeze.

VI. Stories of Art, Science, and Adventure

Lis on the Rocks by Helene D. Grogan

Blow
Lise Weil

We are all so much more than we think we are.... We are air exhaled by hemlocks, we are water plowed by whales, we are matter born in stars, we are children of deep time. -- Great Tide Rising, Kathleen Dean Moore

It was our last day in Baja. I had come here to spend time with whales. I am not fond of heat and Baja is hot. And truthfully, whales, though I worshipped them from afar, had not been my favourite mammals. Despair drove me to Baja. It was March 2017 and I was still reeling from the elections and what they said about the U.S. and our chances of redeeming ourselves as a species. Could nature recover from our relentless assaults? Was there any reason to hope? I thought the whales might have some wisdom to offer. That I would be travelling with a women's wilderness outfit and a guide who communicated with whales seemed to increase the likelihood of this outcome.

When a blue whale first approached – we were camped on the shore of the Sea of Cortez, just gathering for our morning circle—all the other women fell to their knees and stayed there as we watched her circle the bay (a mama and her calf our guide told us). In circle, the women spoke in tones of reverence and rapture. I abstained. I had seen those huge bodies blowing and breaching and yes it was impressive, they were BIG (the biggest mammals on the face of the earth, we had been informed, up to two city blocks in length), and these enormous creatures had come to us, or so the others insisted, come repeatedly, but I felt nothing.... certainly by contrast with my companions. Or, to be honest, I felt rage. What the fuck makes you think they are coming for us? Why the fuck would they want to come to us? After what we've done to them? Done to the oceans. I said this one night around the campfire, my face wet with tears which in all honesty were probably less tears of shame for our species than pain at not being able to feel what the others felt, at feeling separate from them.

But after five days on the Sea of Cortez, spying one fluke after another, watching those giant bodies dive and surface and dive again, I had come to believe, I can't say how exactly, that maybe yes they did love us and yes they had come for us....

Now we were staying in cabins on San Ignacio Bay on the other side of the peninsula. San Ignacio is a protected lagoon where humans can venture out in boats and be pretty sure that they'll not only see but be able to touch a gray whale…One time what looked like a whole pod came and stirred the waters beside our boat, rolling over and spyhopping and cavorting while we raced from side to side of the boat in anticipation. At some point we knew at least one of them would sidle up to us.

I can still feel it, seeing one of those huge mottled gray bodies arcing and diving and arcing again until she was just alongside the boat, how alive it would get down in my belly…In these moments there is only body, there is just you and your friends on this boat and beside you now practically rubbing up against the gunwales, this giant gray slippery body of the "baby" who is the biggest animal you have ever touched. There is only the feel of the slick rubbery skin against your hand as the body moves up and down, the feel of your hand inside the baby's mouth when you manage to push past the soft fringe of the baleen and he seems to grip onto it, the feel of that rubbery skin against your lips the one time you manage to attach your mouth to it…

And now it's our last day. I am going out one more time in the afternoon. As the boat pulls out I wonder if I'm being greedy. I notice myself beginning to long…. to hanker. To crave. Please whales just one last time. As if I haven't already had enough. As if they haven't already given me…. EVERYTHING! Oh but this is my last day, my last chance. Please mama please baby… at last, yes!!! Just fifty feet from our boat, a mama and her large calf, frolicking, seeming to want our company. And now the baby is right up against the boat and the others are all rushing to one side to stroke him—no doubt jonesing like me. Most of them manage to get their hands on him, but he shoots off before I can insinuate myself. Damn! But now… a giant body moving towards us. The mama? Yes! Just feet away!!

We have been sending the mother whales our love now for days, we can't help feeling the most aching gratitude to them for the way they keep offering up their young. And now… now I get to thank her with my hands!! I push my way in and extend myself far over the side of the boat….. She is so close just a few more inches and my fingers will make contact…. Instead   !!!!   Sudden shock of spray. Wet salt spray jet spray and now WET hair WET jacket WET pants and even the boat WET now filling with water and your friends and the driver also wet and pointing at you, laughing—you, who, when the shock relents, are laughing the purest loudest most HEARTY laughter of your entire life. Also the longest, as it goes on and on and on…

because this great mama has just sprayed you, has chosen this moment of your readiness your openness to blow on you with all the force of her giant lungs. There is NOTHING now but this and then for hours there is only this… complete abandon to this moment, of laughter…. And love….

I've been a feminist editor and activist for most of my adult life. In addition to battling patriarchy, operating out of a feminist consciousness for me has meant cultivating joy and wholeness of being. What I learned in Baja was that this mission can only be fully accomplished once we enlist the participation of the nonhuman world. If it feels imperative to me at this moment in time that feminist vision encompass more than the social body, that it also be about animal bodies and the body of the earth, this is not only because the fate of these other bodies is so precarious right now. Even more, it is because without those other bodies, without being able to feel them as part of us, we are so much smaller, so much less powerful, so much less capable of love, and laughter and joy.

Oceans of Love
G.A. Bradshaw

Antarctic seas have a sound and silence of their own. Biologists call animals living in this frigid realm, "extremophiles." The cold daunts even evolution. Compared to African plains and Amazonian jungles, mammalian species in the Antarctic are few. But, what the Antarctic may lack in species numbers is made up by intensity.

Perhaps nowhere is this intensity greater than in the form of a leopard seal. Outside whales, leopard seals are second only in size to the gigantic elephant seal. They are huge. Whether cantering on the ice or undulating under water, leopard seals weigh in at nearly a half ton, wielding their immense, dense bodies with power and precision. Their size and steel-strong jaws, lined with points of ivory, have garnered them a reputation as fierce and intolerant "top predators."

Similar to other carnivores, leopard seals are maligned not only because of what they do for a living – eat other animals – but they can (but don't) eat humans. It is the potentiality, not actuality, that garners leopard seals their negative reputation.

Leopard seal notoriety is not helped by video footage showing hulking, salivating seals in pursuit of helpless penguins or by their visage when, in the face of uncertain strangers, the seal's benevolent, warm and fuzzy, perpetual smile suddenly transforms into a giant, gaping teeth-ringed maw. It was this uneasy mystery surrounding the seal which drew Paul Nicklen and Swedish colleague, photographer Göran Ehlmé, to the Antarctic.

Nicklen is an underwater photographer. Almost daily, he forsakes the open sky to inhabit the planet's breathless skin. Of all the oceans he frequents, his favorite is the shockingly cold waters of the southern pole. Underwater photography is neither straightforward nor easy. Beyond the limitations imposed by a watery world on the land-born, working with submarine subjects has its ethical challenges. Most methods for entering the subsurface world are disruptive. Motorized boats tear at the ocean's tender flesh, driving engine noise into sea life cells and bodies and while subtler, divers insert themselves, uninvited, into private lives and homes.

Nicklen appreciates the importance of honoring animal needs and makes a point of photographing with the caveat, "I want to get close, but I also never want to harass an animal." His camera work benefits from this ethic of humility. In the role of guest, visitors are more likely to see their subjects at ease, engaged in their daily routines uninterrupted by the worry of human intrusion. Charlie Russell, who lived shoulder to shoulder in grizzly bear society for most of his seventy some years, agrees. A quiet demeanor is requisite. "Being with animals, you have to have a certain nonchalance – that's the main ingredient. It makes meeting an animal a non-event."

In this instance, Nicklen wasn't given much time for nonchalance or humility. Immediately after plunging into the ice-floe dotted sea, he was met with a leopard seal's cavernous mouth rushing toward him, stopping only inches away. Her gaping maw nearly covered his mask and camera. "She opened up her mouth and her head is twice as big as a grizzly bear, and I am staring down her throat." As quickly as she had appeared, the seal disappeared, leaving Nicklen wide-eyed, wondering and watching the immense form melt into blue.

The diver was relieved to find that the seal seemed to have satisfied any concern she might have had. But, he soon learned that she wasn't done. To her mind, their initial acquaintance was the first note in a much grander composition. Within moments, the seal returned carrying something, someone, in her mouth - food. The seal had brought the diver food.

The urbanized, humanized world can be unappreciative of the blood and bone of the sustenance upon which we rely. Food has devolved to an elective commodity of taste, entertainment, and convenience. But, in the world of the wild, food is life's essential currency. Every being is aware of its shape and shadow of existence. They understand that they, too, are destined for consumption. It is this knowledge that threads even the most dramatic events by restraint. Killing for food is metered by need, and need alone. On this occasion, the seal's choice of food was penguins.

Swimming up to Nicklen, the leopard seal pushed a frantic penguin toward him. When the diver did not respond, the seal tried again with a second penguin, then again, and again. "She had just caught a penguin chick — she was holding it by the feet — and the penguin is flapping, trying to get away from her. And she would sort of line it up with me, and when it was lined up perfectly with me she would let it go, and it would swim off, she caught it, she did this over and over."

It was obvious that the seal had no hostile intentions. Strange as it seemed, Nicklen realized that the seal was showing concern for his welfare. Notwithstanding high tech gear, a human in the frigid, temperamental waters of the Antarctic is vulnerable. "I think she realized quickly in this encounter that I was not capable of catching a live, moving, swimming penguin, and so she brought me another penguin. She did all these different attempts to feed me live penguins."

Nicklen was stunned. Close encounters are not unusual for veteran divers like Nicklen and Ehlmé. Whales, dolphins, and other seals often approach, accompany, and even play with humans who venture to unnatural depths. But, the encounter with the leopard seal was different. She was not acting in any way he had seen or experienced before. Not only did the seal make several attempts to provide the diver with penguins, she continued to do so every day he dove.

Nicklen's tense excitement is captured in his emotionally charged telling and Ehlmé's vivid imagery. We feel the stalking cold, hear the raspy breath through the ventilator mouthpiece, and watch, with equal awe, as an enormous, looming spotted seal materializes inches away in the icy murk. "All of a sudden here's a top predator, and not only are you getting to see it, it's interacting with you; it's trying to force-feed you penguins, it's trying to take care of you. It's a very, very humbling thing. . . Just to flop yourself into its world and for it to spend that much time and energy trying to figure out who you are and to interact with you."

For most humans, seeing a dolphin, seal, or orca is exciting, but little thought is given to what it takes to survive. Although the seal made multiple trips in fairly quick order to supply the diver with additional penguins, her efforts entailed a lot of work. Their sessions together lasted four days. As Nicklen underscored, four calorie-expensive days used for someone else's welfare is notable. No matter how powerful someone is or how plentiful food may be, any distraction from the job of staying alive is risky. Wildlife runs on a thin margin. Injury, a missed meal, and inattention easily spiral into disaster and death. Evolutionary biology understands Nature as a strict bookkeeper who keeps tally to ensure that life's equation of costs and benefits balance out. There are diverse dimensions to Nature's spreadsheet. Every action and every relationship has psychological, social, and physical consequences, all of which affect a living being.

In the eyes of Charles Darwin and friends, Nicklen posed more of a liability than any advantage. The time that the leopard seal spent with the diver put her short- and long-term survival budget in the red. Nicklen was neither a member of the seal nor local marine communities, so there was no genetic, cross-generational gain or collateral payoff. Even if he wanted to, being so ungainly in the marine world, the diver could not reciprocate or offer the seal protection, food, or advantage. He was a transient guest without community ties, earth bound and bound to leave for good. On top of this, he was human, a species that has caused thousands upon thousands of seal deaths in the course of plundering the oceans for fat, flesh, and fur. Although other seal and whale species may have been hit harder than "sea leopards," no one forgets the terror of exploding harpoons and guns and blue waters turned red.

Given this perspective, we are compelled to expand the aperture of analysis to understand what seems to fly in the face of traditional theories of behavior and biology. Nature abhors illogic as much as vacuums. All of the evidence, and theory, suggest that something else must be involved. The most parsimonious and obvious explanation is what Nicklen himself surmised: the seal was trying to help. The diver might have felt well within the range of safety, but given the length of time and effort measured in penguins alone, the leopard seal exhibited a heartfelt desire to aid someone who, in her mind, was literally out of his depth. Even so, why was helping this man so important? What purpose could it serve the seal?

Neuroscience asserts that while details of seal and human brains may be tailored in unique ways to navigate their respective environments and needs, both species share fundamental emotional tendencies and affective systems. The leopard seal's sympathetic offerings are consistent with what brain science predicts: seals and other animals have the capacity to care for one and another. Even though a human was the recipient of her care, it is within psychobiological expectations that the seal would reach out. It is not unusual that animals extend consideration to kith as well as kin.

Conventionally, leopard seals have been regarded as an exception to the rule of care. Much like their frightening reputation as ask-no-questions vicious killers, the image of leopard seals as selfish solitaries is also incorrect. Along with pumas, who are similarly labelled asocial loners, seals spend more time with each other than supposed. Both participate in "cooperative hunting" and share food with family and friends. They may not travel in close knit herds as do elk and elephants, but pumas and leopard seals are part of an active, connected culture.

Neither is it unusual for an animal to come to the aid of a human in distress. There are innumerable instances when an animal has put his life on the line for someone unrelated. This had a powerful effect on the diver. Through the seal's enlistment, Nicklen was dislodged from his usual role of observer to become the observed, a co-participant in an unfolding, profoundly emotional experience. The sudden reversal from subject to object catapulted Nicklen to a realm beneath the material offerings of penguins, a place where, even in the silence of the sea, he heard the seal's deep care. "It's embarrassing to admit this. . . I'd fall asleep at night with tears coming down my cheeks. . I was just so grateful." Yet, it is unfair to both seal and penguin to regard the sacrificed birds as merely units of food. Seals and other carnivores do not kill wantonly. Innumerable observations, such as a video showing an African leopard trying to care for an infant baboon whose mother the leopard had just killed, attest to carnivores' appreciation and of understanding the sacredness of life.

As time went on, the seal's involvement increased. When efforts to feed the diver continued to fail, the seal's concern turned into impatient frustration. "She got so tired of me being unable to accept one of her penguins that she grabbed it and she flipped it on top of my head." Nicklen also became increasingly engaged. "I think that's why I get emotional, because we had such a connection."

His use of "connection" in lieu of "interaction" is telling. Similar to "transaction," which characterizes an exchange of material or nonmaterial goods, "interaction" focuses on what goes on between two people – in this case, the transactional component was penguins. "Connection," on the other hand, focuses less on one person or the other - or even the stuff in between. It is the recognition of the steady state in which we all live – the underlying unity beneath the multitudinous.

Nicklen's descriptions are akin to those which take us out of time to a space of being where separation between self and other disappears—the space of love. He makes this very confession. "I definitely fell in love with this seal." Through a series of interactions, a flash encounter suddenly morphed into a relationship compelled by genuine compassion.

Compassion draws from a fenceless space. It is different from altruism because compassion comes from an understanding of being connected. True compassion does not stop where one body ends and another begins. In this space of wholeness, the sense of individual identity fades away. There is an unconditional acceptance for the wellbeing of another.

Similar to the Little Mermaid in Hans Christian Anderson's tale who risked her life for the drowning young prince, the leopard seal expressed a moral commitment to walk, or in this case, swim, beside another through life's ups and downs. The leopard seal lent her personal currency to support someone she perceived was in need. The seriousness of her investment is reflected in the length of time she spent with Nicklen and her growing emotional intensity. This was no passing whim.

On no occasion throughout the entire half week did the seal falter. She met up with him every day and showed an unwavering willingness, almost desperation, to do what she believed was needed to help him. "At one point . . there's a photo of her looking dejected, sort of disappointed in me that I'm so useless that I'm unable to catch or accept one of her gifts, so then she started to bring me dead penguins, and at one point I had five penguins floating around my head." Her search for the perfect penguin ceased only when Nicklen signaled, by leaving for good, that her task was complete. The diver returned home, changed. "What you learn about these animals is how communicative they are, how intelligent they are, how social they are, how forgiving they are."

The seal's inclusive ethos of compassion, the commitment to a greater good beyond the personal, is a cherished quality found in many human spiritual traditions and indigenous cultures. Andean Quechua live by an ethos of oneness or nonduality, an understanding that there is seamless connectivity binding together all life. In these worldviews, personal identity exists, but it is regarded as merely a thread in the vast fabric of Nature's wholeness. When Justo Oxa, a schoolteacher from the region, says, "I am not from Huantura, I am Huantura," he is describing how Quechuan identity is inextricably bound to the entirety of where and with whom he lives, the mountains, streams, people - everything and everyone. This view of humanity's uninterrupted relationship with the rest of Nature is also resonant with western science.

Since the discovery of quantum phenomena over one hundred years ago, nondualism has subsumed dualism with a series of theories across disciplines. Mathematics' complexity and chaos theories, psychology's attachment theory, and biology's epigenetics are all relationally based where objects of study are not individual components, but the processes and spaces connecting them. It is the synergy of inheritance and experience which is important, not one or the other. It is the nature and type of local interactions, not individual agents, which are responsible for creating emergent properties, and it was the leopard seal's inclusive compassion which brought the diver from the cold into her sphere of warming care.

The seal was expressing the innate understanding of what quantum physicist David Bohm referred to as wholeness. Caring for another, even when it may appear costly to the giver, does not run counter to the mandate of personal preservation. Nature has found a way of seamlessly retaining wholeness while reveling in life's dazzling diversity. The seal's efforts to aid the diver were not the act of one individual coming to the aid of another - they were gestures of someone reaching out to herself.

Literature cited
Bradshaw, G.A. (2020). *Talking with Bears: Conversations with Charlie Russell*. Rocky Mountain Books.

Bradshaw, G. A. (2017). *Carnivore minds: Who these fearsome animals really are*. Yale University Press.

Gross, T. (2017). Photographer shares his view of a ferocious but fragile ecosystem. Fresh Air, June 6, 2017. https://www.npr.org/2017/06/06/531735345/polar-photographer-shares-his-view-of-a-ferocious-but-fragile-ecosystem; retrieved 16 October 2019.

Owen-Smith, N., & Chafota, J. (2012). Selective feeding by a megaherbivore, the African elephant (*Loxodonta africana*). Journal of Mammalogy, 93(3), 698-705.

Robbins, J.R., Poncet, D., Evans, A.R. and Hocking, D.P., 2019. A rare observation of group prey processing in wild leopard seals (*Hydrurga leptonyx*). Polar Biology, 42(8), pp.1625-1630.

The Ember
Rebecca R Burrill

Stepping off the shack's four-foot-wide deck into the deep overgrown pathway of salt spray roses, and winding up past the privy and onto the crest of the rise, I find myself in the presence of a 360-degree unfathomable expanse of undulating dunes and ocean. The early morning is dark and heavy with a somber stillness after three days of high gale winds and rain.

I have not yet unshuttered the windows, nor untacked the blanketed creviced and disjointed door of the one room shack. But in waiting the three days to complete my assignment—that of sensory immersion languaging with Place—I emerge from the low horizontal south window onto the shack's deck with anticipation.

I am headed for the dune hollow previously visited on the first day of my residency, about which I wrote a poem:

DUNE HOLLOW
Circle
Of surround
Hollow of beach plums
Rising to the sky
      Undulus circumference

Disk
Of low western sun
A single penetrating eye
    Enshrouded
        With concentric circles
           Of shimmering
              Grey-blue haze

Hawk
Lifts above the rise—hovering
Sharp angled
    Cutting to the east
      Riding the full damp strength
         Of North East wind

But during the three day sequester, I reread my residency proposal written months earlier, and renew my original purpose. I ponder this while descending from my 360-degree perch, weaving around one dune and then another, entering Dune Hollow to re-encounter this Place through immersion languaging. I meet Dune Hollow as a community of animate, communicative Beings.

Senses immersed and perceptions heightened in radical receptivity of Place, I allow myself to be spoken with by the myriad languaging gestures of the present Beings—qualities of movements, sounds, textures, volumes, weights, shapes, colors, intensities, forces, feelings, moods, intimations, depths, and more. I respond through the fundamental of all languaging—movement and sound gesture: dance and song. I find myself in an immediate and spontaneous conversation—an improvisational flow of qualities in perpetual call and response, as eternal in this moment as all of creation.

I feel cradled in this rhythmical reciprocation. I am a participant in an olden way of knowing and being, a fully embodied and embedded member of the immediate community of Earth in this particle Place in this particular Moment. I come to stillness. I rest in ceremonial gratitude and acknowledgment.

From this dance of communion, I write my poem of encounter, which flows from me as avidly as the dance itself:

DUNE HOLLOW IMMERSION DANCE
Dune Hollow
Holding Womb

My womb
Holding containing
Stillness holding
Containing containing
Wind breeze
    Wind zephyrs
        Wind blows
            Wind undulations
                Wind bound and free rhythms
    Wind playing amongst your children

The grasses and seaside goldenrod and bayberry
Roses blooming in the 1st week of October
Fierce holding
Gentle holding
The mother the womb
Nurturing sustaining
Mother holding—strong, unmoving

Mosses
Grass tufts and
Rosehips
Mottled grey cloud puffs
      Low lying next to you
And beach plums

My womb your womb
Giving-taking
Living-dying
Closing in on the central fire
The womb
The seed
That never dies
The ember
Carried quietly in the ember pot
Holding in me—I die I close up I rest

The seed
Quiet
      No sign of life
The womb carries
Quiet flame
Suddenly ready; suddenly change

The womb growing
    Opens forth
        A new one
        A new child
            A new womb
                To grow and become
                A giver

         A stander
         A dancer
         A wise woman
    Who releases more
         More holding
            More
           For you

These two poems express different human orientations toward Nature. The first is a about a place. The second is of a communicative interrelationship with the animate intelligences of Place. Through this communicative interrelationship we can be informed of deep olden ways of knowing and participating with the mystery of the womb of creation—as Kin. This is in contrast to human separatist positioning of dominion/domination over Nature. The experiential recognition of this difference can be a healing ember for the psychosis of this separatist rift; a healing ember for the pervasive ecocide of our times.

Mountain Meditation
Leo Hwang

Hitchiking around the Irish countryside with my backpack I didn't have a tent, but a tarp that I set up under my sleeping bag under the stars on clear nights, and when it rained, I rolled myself inside like a burrito. I had a small candle lantern for light, so for the most part, when the sun went down, I went to sleep, and when the sun rose, I woke to start my day.

This is the time in my life as when I was most physically in tune with the planet, my circadian rhythms at one with my surroundings. I moved from landscape to landscape primarily by bipedal locomotion. I carried a bottle and ate mostly cheese and bread. My rhythms were like the sheep that milled about in the dawn, and fell silent at dusk.

That was many years ago now, but these days I find unexpected moments of connection to nature. Seeing an eagle flying overhead while driving. Or in the creak of the soon-to-collapse tree strung up with vines just a little distance into woods off the driveway. Or maybe in the way the wind blows and leans against the house like a dear friend.

It seems to me that honoring nature has more to do with notebooks and pens, and less to do with phones and digital images. There is something insufficient in our seeking to capture the moment with a video or picture --the translation into pixels, into two dimensions, the limitations of aperture, the absence of sound or smell, temperature, and the touch of leaves and spiderwebs. Perhaps more so during the pandemic, there is a need for the real thing, not the facsimile.

Connecting with nature is mostly a solitary thing, something like meditation. But I also recognize that some of the most deeply felt moments in nature have been with a friend, a partner, who is able to also honor nature, to slow down and sit silently, to let it all soak into one's soul the way smoke permeates one's clothes, until your very skin is smeared with and tastes like nature.

Hiking in Glacier National Park with colleagues I met at a conference, we sat resting on an outcropping of rock extending out into Lake MacDonald. The crisp spring air was too loud coming down off the mountains to hear one another, and the wind threatened to carry us off the cliff if we were too careless. We each sat in our respective stations staring out into the distance, feeling the stone beneath us, the curling fingers of glacial wind reaching in the seams of our jackets and touching the skin at the nape of our necks and down across our chests as if we were naked and wore nothing at all. It was an awesome moment where we suddenly understood what it means to be alive, what it meant to share our existence together on this planet, and how significant our insignificance was.

Tree of Souls (*Avatar*)
Joan Maloof

The Tree of Souls is a giant willow-like tree in the fantasy film *Avatar*. The film, written and directed by James Cameron in 2009, describes contact with the fictional Na'vi people. The Tree of Souls is the most sacred thing that exists for the Na'vi people. It is their direct connection to Eywa (what they call their Supreme Being). The tree is able to connect with the nervous system of the Na'vi people, and it can also connect them all together as one. If the tree were to be destroyed, it would create a cultural and spiritual void that would destroy the race. Thus, it is also called the "home tree." The tree produces seeds that look like a cross between a huge dandelion seed and a small jellyfish. The seeds drift slowly and playfully. But the seeds are more than just genetic material for trees; they are pure and sacred spirits, known as woodsprites. So, if a seed from the tree chooses to land on a spot, it is considered an auspicious sign. When someone from the tribe dies, a woodsprite is planted with them; in that way the deceased stays connected to Eywa and the rest of the tribe.

The Tree of Souls resonated with moviegoers. It reflected the beliefs of ancient cultures across the globe, such as Druids and Native Americans, who revere certain trees and refuse to cut them. In 2010, in Hyde Park, London, an interactive replica of the Tree of Souls was installed. The fiber-optic cables it was made from could change colors, move to music, and display uploaded messages. A consortium of groups, including 20th Century Fox, committed to planting a real tree for every person who interacted with the sculptural tree. This Avatar Home Tree Initiative funded the planting of more than a million trees across the globe.

Perhaps the closest thing to a real-life Tree of Souls is the Lone Poplar (*Populus laurifolia*) in the Kalmykia province of southwest Russia. This tree is "lone" because it is the only tree for many miles. The surrounding landscape is a vast grassland. How did the tree get there? The story of its origin tells of a Buddhist monk who made a pilgrimage to Tibet and then stored some seeds from his journey in his walking staff. When he returned he hiked to the highest mound on the vast, empty steppe. He planted his staff in that spot and eventually the seeds sprouted. In what century did that happen? The identity of the monk and the year of the planting are both unknown. As the tree got larger, travelers on long horseback journeys would stop in the shade of the tree for a rest. As they rested they brought their requests to the tree. The requests were granted. More people came to pray and worship at the tree; these were no longer travelers just passing through but spiritual pilgrims coming specifically to worship at the tree. Today the tree is regarded as a shrine, and visitors by the hundreds bring prayer flags and incense to the tree and pray and meditate in its presence.

The Voices Return
Christian McEwen

> *In a bittersweet twist, the surreal slowdown of life as we know it has presented researchers with a rare opportunity to study the modern world under some truly bizarre conditions...*
>
> --- Marina Koren

Janey Winter lives by herself on the borders of Provincetown. A year-round resident and working artist, she has known the place for more than sixty years. But soon after the coronavirus lockdown, she heard something utterly new from her back porch — "a big long roar — a horizontal roar — that beat below everything — a cosmic sound." It was, of course, the Atlantic Ocean, always, till now, obscured by the churn of the daily traffic. "I couldn't believe it," Winter told me. The following month it was written up in the local paper. "Even people in town could hear it!" But she herself had noticed it much earlier — two full weeks ahead of the editorial — and was gleefully delighted by that fact.

Similar discoveries are being made across the globe, as planes are grounded, cruises canceled, trains and buses set to run less frequently. The family car sits idle in the driveway. Motor-bikes are stalled. Ordinary vibrations caused by human activity (biking, running, walking, even shopping) have been reduced to almost nil. And with that comes an unprecedented opportunity to listen.

"I used to think there weren't really birds in Wuhan," wrote Rebecca Franks on her Facebook page, "because you rarely saw them and never heard them." In fact, they had simply been drowned out by the relentless human traffic. NPR correspondents Eleanor Beardsley and Sylvia Poggioli both had similar stories. Beardsley had heard egrets on the Seine for the first time ever, and Poggioli (based in Rome) had been taken aback by the sheer volume of the dawn chorus. That avian orchestra, proclaiming spring, was for her, she said, "almost too loud."

With human noise on pause, seismologists, naturalists, and other professional listeners have been seizing the chance to record how Earth sounds, uninterrupted. In the U.K., seismologist Paula Koelemeijer was happy to learn that a 5.5 magnitude earthquake (usually inaudible) could suddenly be heard in Central London. Across Europe, the Silent Cities project has called forth an army of volunteers (scientists, journalists, artists and interested amateurs), eager to track "the little sounds of every day" — from bees nuzzling deep into scented blossoms to tiny beetles foraging about among the leaves.

For years now, too many of us have been moving through the world in a daze of our own making. We have grown oblivious to the voices of the birds and the trees, the mountains and the rivers. As Thomas Berry puts it, "We have broken the great conversation," thoughtlessly inured to talking only to ourselves.

But as lockdown continues, and the voices filter back, that conversation has a chance to be repaired. Deprived of their usual work-outs at the gym, people begin to walk outside more regularly, enjoying the natural benefits (less stress, lowered blood-pressure, more and better sleep), whilst also responding to the ambient sound. A friend in the Scottish Highlands reports on a pair of cuckoos calling back and forth across the glen (the male higher, the female lower, throatier). Neighbors in Vermont remark on the shrill of the spring peepers, the creak and sway of the tall pines. Birdsong seems notably louder, more widespread. With human traffic so drastically reduced, birds no longer have to raise their voices to compete with cars and trucks. They can focus on courtship, on providing for their nestlings. They are able, very literally, to sleep in. It seems likely that 2020 will be a bonanza year for birds: with larger, healthier broods and more relaxed and happier parents.

With luck, that ease of being can extend to us as well. At some point as yet unknown to us, COVID-19 will be contained, and the usual human racket will return. Meanwhile, we can relish the opportunity to slow down and pay attention, not just to the chatter in our heads, but to all the other myriad sounds. Because if these last weeks have taught us anything it's that the natural world has plenty to say for itself — from the scurrying of insects to that rich, deep ocean roar — and all we have to do is stop and listen.

Williamsburg, MA, April 2020

Every River Wants to Flow
Susan Cerulean

If you examine a satellite photo of north Florida's panhandle between Bald Point and Panama City, your eye cannot miss the channel that has delivered our shoreline's beaches, bars and barrier islands. Hundreds of millions of years ago, mountains as tall and rugged as the Sawtooth Range of the Idaho Rockies rose from the footprint of the Appalachian Mountains. Over unimaginably long eons, those granite peaks weathered into milky white quartz and dark feldspar and sluiced down two rivers, the Chattahoochee and the Flint. At their confluence, the Apalachicola carried the mountains' sediment down to the Gulf of Mexico, where she opened like a fist, punching through her own accumulations, growing out the land. In this way, the River collaborated with the Gulf of Mexico and the rising sea to create islands, a precious island chain. When you cup a handful of white sand from one of our beaches in the palm of your hand, you hold the bodies of mountains.

The River carries in the green muscle of her body, a sweet freshwater flow, the sum of the rivers pouring into her body (the Flint and Chattahoochee and Chipola and East), and their attendant creeks, and bayous, and sloughs, and springs and lakes, as well (Owl and Spring and Graham and Cash and Whiskey George). Think of all those waters blending and surrendering themselves into one. Think of how each of creek and bayou and slough surrenders name and individual identity. And then, how the Apalachicola herself dives into the Gulf of Mexico, and seems to be lost. Now think of how that water rises again and again as fog and cloud, and is eventually reborn as rain.

***

I recently dreamed that I came to the bank of the Apalachicola River and all that remained of north Florida's mightiest watercourse was a cracked and muddy channel, a tragedy of epic proportions.
I know it's possible, for I have seen a river turned ghost.

***

If you fly to Los Angeles, your final minutes take you over the San Gabriel mountains and then down into the Los Angeles basin, where a great river once ran.

The Los Angeles River gathered waters from an underground aquifer in the San Fernando Valley and from the surrounding mountains, nourishing a lush coastal plain. Today, she is largely encased in concrete and barely recognizable as a river. In 1934, after a devastating New Year's Day flood, Congress authorized the Army Corps of Engineers to tame the Los Angeles. They deepened her channel and encased three-quarters of her length in a concrete ditch.

Trafficked by our takings, the Los Angeles has become an irrigation canal, a "water freeway," a narrow ribbon of water running at the base of gray concrete slabs. That is what you will see from the windows of your descending airplane. But you can also see that it's not the River that is broken, but rather the human relationship to her that has caused the near death of this ancient waterway.

The Los Angeles River holds a vision for herself, and waits for her waters to be returned. Waits for her needs to be honored so that she may again breathe in and out, up-and-down, with seasonal rainfall and even tidal movement, as all coastal rivers are born to do.

***

The Apalachicola is not yet a ghost.

But a version of my nightmare, and Los Angeles River's reality, looms. Her waters are shrinking. Her own bay, her own glorious glittering mouth, no longer delivers the blend of fresh water needed to nourish her once famous nursery of fish and shrimp and oysters and crabs.

In Florida, we blame the mining of the River's water on Atlanta, on that city's concrete explosion of growth, on lawns and golf courses, and the reservoir called Lake Lanier, and all the ways people can think of to slacken their industrial thirst. Further south, as she passes through Georgia, people want the Apalachicola to irrigate field crops and pecan groves, to supply chicken farms and paper mills.

But it is not for the sentient River's sake alone that Florida sends its governor to parry and fence with the governors and courts of Georgia and Alabama. Our seafood harvests are not asphalt and cotton, but our claim is the same kind of claim.

***

Some people may think of the River as inanimate. But when we look deeply, we can see that this is not mere water, not simply a set of commodites. She has her own intelligence and has created a setting where millions of plants and animals thrive, in her channels, in her floodplains, and in her Bay. In the embrace of her warm, mocha estuary, generations of oyster larvae rooted themselves on layers upon layers of shell, thriving on the nutrients delivered from deepest Georgia. Here, beings beyond count or calculation have arisen, lived, died, and dissolved, their shells and bones and teeth and fins and stems sliding back into the Bay and the Gulf.

The River is not an object. The River is not yet a ghost.

***

If we did assume that the River and her occupants: oysters, sturgeon, swallow-tailed kites, floodplain forests, kingfishers--if we assume they are just a collection of objects, then we would believe they have no moral standing. In fact, it does not matter whether we think a particular species or river is important or natural or beautiful. We did not create them, and we do not own them. The truth is that the Earth's creations have intention, agency, worth and rights, far beyond what we humans ascribe to them.

Visionary cultural historian Thomas Berry observed that humans created the concept of rights—and then awarded them all, to themselves. And that is the deep pathology of our time: to consider our rights as human beings to be different from those of the rest of creation. This leads us to believe that we may take whatever we like, and it also lulls into thinking that our future is unrelated to the fate of the rivers, the shorebirds, or the islands.

The Apalachicola is immense, beautiful, precious and unique. Rocking on her current, we feel her power—taut and muscular and green, brown and warm and welcoming. She is not yet a ghost, but she is troubled by our takings. A just apportionment of the Apalachicola must be based on the inborn rights of her extraordinarily complex web of life, as well, before our own desires. It comes down to this: We have to change our human relationship to the River. We are required to separate our needs from our wants, and to rein in the consumptive mindset that dominates our culture.

Finding Hope in a Web of Mutuality
Deb Habib

There is a crate of potatoes in front of me and I am gently brushing off the soil. It is quiet where I stand on our farm. I look up through the low translucent roof of the shed above me, dappled with brown red yellow autumn leaves. When an acorn hits it, the gong of fall resonates. With potatoes, a little soil left on is good. It's better not to wash it off, but to let them rest in it then lightly remove most of it. I think, and I enjoy thinking about how a light cover of remaining soil rich with microbes offers some protective shield to the potatoes in storage through the winter. I like to ingest just a bit of soil from the crops grown on our land now and then-- not enough for the crunch to disrupt the pleasure of some creamy mashed or roasted with garlic potatoes, but just enough to let some beneficial microbes enter my body and add to the plethora of others working it out in my biome. With the soil, some embodied sunshine, the rains, the decay of organic matter and the good work of my husband's farmer hands also enter my being. We've come to know the soil on our farm by watching it build, layer by layer. Most often soil is an outcome of hundreds of years of action below the surface, but ours has been more rapidly built from what happens above the surface.

When we were looking for a place to root, raise our family and a farm for livelihood, there was no way we could have afforded 'typical' farmland, flat or along rivers, and with feet of topsoil. In the end it has been so good, as we had to work with what we had with a focus on creating rather than extracting. We layered organic materials- cardboard, mulch, compost- and we still do, year after year. We didn't till and turn with tractors because there was nothing to go down into- so we focused on building it up. We watched as life flourished. The soil became abundant with earthworms and their rich castings, webs of mycorrhizal fungi wherever we looked, and the knowing that there was microscopic yet essential life in this now remarkably fertile soil.

The potato crop of red, golden, and blue gems was unearthed from narrow rows that were gently hilled over many months with adjacent soil and mulch hay. Brushing off the potato soil, I recall the planting. With the pandemic spring of 2020 requiring even more farm energy than usual to navigate and to meet demand for fresh food, we didn't have a moment to think about potatoes until a bit late, when apples were in blossom. With the surge in new gardeners due to COVID-19 keeping people home, farm supply stores sold out of many varieties of seed potatoes before we could get some. One day

I was waiting to pay for my groceries at our beloved community food coop, Quabbin Harvest. The six foot distancing in the line put me right beside the rack of slightly dated, reduced price fruits and veggies. And lo and behold, on that shelf was a nice bin of just starting to sprout blue potatoes, my favorite! Organic and sufficiently local, they would be perfectly good for the needed seed. With this low-cost bounty in my back seat, I was reminded of what has guided much of our farming ways at Seeds of Solidarity: creativity, and keeping our eyes open to the many human and natural resources that exist in one's community.

Our farm methods and the small community food coop resemble and reflect elements of an ecosystem. In a healthy ecosystem, each organism serves a role and interacts to benefit the whole. We've observed this on our farm where, with no choice but to see what happened when we layered organic resources with minimal disturbance, soil life self-organized with increased vitality and fertility a wonderful result. A food cooperative is an organized structure, but at its best, the principles of collaboration and community benefit resemble ecosystem thinking. In a corporate grocery setting, a box of sprouting potatoes would not likely be visible and available near the checkout counter to be found by a worker-member like me, such as happened at our small food cooperative. In further illustration of the ecosystem model, prior to shopping I had just finished a coop volunteer shift helping to pack weekly shares of vegetables for low-income families in our community, vegetables from local farmers who came to rely increasingly on the sales from this small coop given the fallout of other markets due to COVID-19 upheavals.

Our community is low-wealth and rural. I was not born here but have been here over 20 years, longer than I have lived anywhere else. When we sought land for Seeds of Solidarity farm, good solar access for an off of the grid home and farm, and land affordability were our primary needs. Along with these and the task ahead of carving a life and livelihood out of a long abandoned, small, logged clearing in the woods with thin soil, we landed in a neighborhood filled with very resourceful folks. We have learned much about the capacity for a neighborhood to function in ways that also resemble a healthy ecosystem ripe with mutual benefit. We've learned that we all don't have to know or own everything ourselves, and where a diversity of skills and experiences enrich the whole. The skills and services in a rural neighborhood ecosystem may differ from those in an urban ecosystem, but the potential and increasing necessity to connect in a web of mutual support is common to all communities. In fact, the practice of mutual aid as a reciprocal, voluntary exchange of resources and services rose in 2020 amid, and in response to suffering and injustice exposed by the pandemic. In these times, we see such networks not only rising as isolated responses to emergency needs, but as a form of participation that goes beyond charitable, to actually inform and change conditions and systems that are extractive and unjust. When I think to the future, be it during moments of gently wiping soil from potatoes or other endeavors, nature remains a consistent and inspiring teacher about the power of connection. We are living in times at once tenuous and precious, ripe with possibility. The wisdom of how to move forward in more connected and mutually beneficial ways- like healthy soil- has long been at our feet.

VII. Stories of Faith

Callanish I by Lis McLoughlin

What Is It For?
Cheryl Savageau

But *what is it for?* She asks me as we drive through the forest of tiny trees. They are no more than four feet tall, these high desert trees. They are not babies, they are full grown, like the scrub pines on Cape Cod. I am lost in this nation of trees, on this road somewhere near Taos, New Mexico. I am used to the maples of the Northeast, I walk in their shade. So this is what they call a forest here. I know that's not really true, I've seen the tall pines that grow up at Los Alamos, on the mountain road I drive from Albuquerque to Santa Fe, the road I prefer because they are there. But it pleases me to be amongst this forest of tiny trees, their difference charms me. Any time I travel, I'm afraid I'll get there and it will be unfamiliar, alien, but when I step off the plane, I realize, oh, yes, this is the earth, and take a trusting breath.

She is talking again, and I switch my attention from the Land outside the car to her words. But *what is it for*, she asks again. I don't understand the question. I think maybe I'm not paying close enough attention, distracted as I am by the trees. But it is the trees she is talking about. You know, she says, gesturing with her right hand as she steers with her left. All this. All this, she says, *what is it for?*

What do you mean, *what is it for?*

You know, is it for farming, or dairy, or ranching....you know, *what is it for?*

What is it for? It's for itself, I say. She shakes her head in frustration.

This conversation has become emblematic - those moments of cultural dissonance in so many conversations, when I realize the underpinnings of our conversations are different, that what I think we are talking about is not it at all.

When I was in my twenties, my then-husband's aunt was concerned at what she considered my "atheism." I never said I was an atheist. It's not a word I would use, based on a negative, a lack of something, rather than on a positive presence that I felt but couldn't express. How can you not believe in God? she asked. How do you know what is good or evil? What will you teach your children?

I remember the question being so much bigger than I, at that time in my life, could answer in this short conversation over the kitchen table. I didn't know how to talk about the sacred. I felt instead an abyss, an absence of words, one that led me to become a poet. I could only tell her that I couldn't believe in that personal God, that old man in the sky. There were so many assumptions that we didn't share. I didn't yet know our Abenaki word, Ktsi Niwaskw - that sacred mysterious matrix of being, often translated as "Great Spirit."

What is it for? The language that inhabits her, that inhibits her, says that these trees, this forest are objects. What I see as beings, as a nation of trees, she sees as, not exactly non-living, because she would admit that trees are alive, in a limited way, but they have no sovereignty, no personhood. They exist only in relation to human needs. Which means they are expendable. This place should be "for" something that humans need. Otherwise, what?

I could say that they are "for" making oxygen, that they might hold some medicine that we don't even know about, that they hold together the soil in this arid place and provide food, make a home for a vast population of birds, insects, reptiles, mammals, invertebrates. But that is not what they are "for." These are gifts they give freely. Our proper response is gratitude.

What is it for? She turns on the radio. I look out the window. The Land extends in all its beauty, in all its mystery. This Forest, this Nation.

Walking the Land of the Nailbourne
Simon Wilson

1.
In Old English the verb 'to walk' meant 'to roll' or 'to turn over.' It could be used figuratively, as in 'to turn over in one's mind.'

Walking, we turn over the landscape, and new possibilities, new considerations, new visions, too. As the landscape rolls past, we turn over what we see, what we experience, what we have experienced, and what we will experience. Past, present and future are turned over; they always will have been.
The mind, too, is turned over in the landscape. All is rolled into a complex, involved whole, where mind creates landscape and landscape creates mind, in intricate and endless Celtic knotwork. And who or what is turning over or being turned over is not clear, as all is interwoven: always will have been.

The illuminated letter of a Lindisfarne Gospel is composed of such labyrinthine knotwork. In the third century, St Anthony of the Desert had called the whole of nature a book (which St Cuthbert, seeking his own desert in and beyond Lindisfarne, surely knew). All of nature is an enspirited poem whose divine beauty leads to infinity. Those with eyes to see can read it, and in reading it they too become gods: gods of poetry.

Creation's beauty yearns to be written by those who meet and respond to its longing with their own yearning. Mutual embrace leads to mutual transfiguration, to life itself, always continuing the making of the world and always just at the beginning. Writing the first letter; being written into it. Eternally nearing the freedom of Beginning and Eden.

2.
In East Kent, an obscure corner of England, I was again beginning. At first the landscape of the Elham Valley remained closed. Lovely, but closed. Old folklore was a mark of yearnings, however. I learnt that the intermittent flowing of the valley's little river, the Nailbourne, presages national disaster both material and spiritual: it is one of the five woewaters of England.

Half-way up a hill, and next to the road descending to my village to cross the Nailbourne, is Old England's Hole. Traditionally this is where local tribes dug in, in a last-ditch attempt to resist Caesar and his army in 54BC.

The romance of loss, the erasure of Albion, is in this land. Always happened, always will happen. Longing, too, begins here, for Albion, for Avalon, for Logres. For Eden.

Strangely unsung, this area's appearances in literature are as intermittent as the Nailbourne, and bear the same burden of meaning. Malory, Fleming, Brooke, Hoban. Arthur and Mordred battle on Barham Down, above the river and its valley. James Bond motors our local roads, for England must be saved from Goldfinger and Drax. Their lairs are not tropical islands but Reculver, Sandwich, Kingsdown. Bond himself was brought up in Pett Bottom, just a five-minute drive from Old England's Hole, via the home of author Jocelyn Brooke. Brooke has the Third World War spread from Clambercrown into the Elham Valley and thence through England. Later, Riddley Walker explores this post-apocalyptic land, though the Nailbourne has degenerated into Nelly's Bum.

Here begins the fall of the once and future king, and with him Logres. Bond and Brooke and Hoban too know that England will end here (always will have).

Where the dream of Albion ends it has its beginning. Folklore and fiction know that the land of the Nailbourne yearns to love the poet who, created again, will create it again. And all will hear once more the voice of God walking there.

The Whole Inexpressible Thing
Julia Sibley-Jones

I am nostalgic for the future.

I am already missing the time I won't have with friends we usually see in February. I'm missing my children being at school for the day and then happy to be home. I'm missing all the normal things that continue not to happen and trying to find God in what is happening right now.

Here's what I've noticed. God shows up when I'm looking for God, because God has been there all along, waiting for me to notice. Boundless, creative, playful God who delights in variety and abundance. See if you can find me in this camouflaged frog! Check out me in this purple iris! Watch while I turn that whole hillside golden. And don't forget the people! Look at me looking at you through this stranger's eyes. See me in that boy pushing past boredom in online learning, that first-grade girl researching the Statue of Liberty. I'm here in that warrior recovering from surgery, that woman insisting that no-one underestimate her students, that colleague digging deep to deliver on time. The miracles are everywhere.

I notice a lot on my walks.

Once I found the beautiful yellow body of a turtle the size of a silver dollar. Twice under a bridge I've seen a snake with its slim, lithe body swaying in the current like the snagged branches it was under. Many times, I've discovered blue-tailed skinks in tree stumps.

The adult male *Plestiodon fasciatus* has a red head and neck and less distinct lines on his back. The juveniles have five dark lines and blue tails, to keep territorial males from attacking them. I've enjoyed catching them sunning themselves or hiding in the crevices of the stumps. It's probably not mutual, but I like knowing their address and feel a new connection with their limited-radius habitat. I've been on the lookout for their southern cousin *Plestiodon inexpectatus*—but if I see one it will, indeed, be unexpected.

While I walk, I listen to inspirational or funny podcasts. No news analysis or self-help or current events. I often laugh out loud, which is such a gift. Plus, since everyone's kinda crazy right now, no one looks at me strangely when I laugh out loud.

After discovering Conan O'Brien's podcast, I watched the commencement address he gave at Dartmouth College in 2011. This is wonderful advice.

> It is our failure to become our perceived ideal that ultimately defines us and makes us unique. It's not easy, but if you accept your misfortune and handle it right, your perceived failure can become a catalyst for profound re-invention. Whether you fear it or not, disappointment will come. The beauty is that through disappointment you can gain clarity, and with clarity comes conviction and true originality. Work hard, be kind, and amazing things will happen.

As we know, those amazing things may turn out to be inexpectatus.

We are all living through a season of disappointment. What will we do with this opportunity? I want us—each individual—to choose to use it as a catalyst for reinvention. As so many people have said, we will not return to 'normal' after this pandemic. The world is irreparably changed. But we have the opportunity to reinvent ourselves. What do we want the future to look like? I want us to restart the economy, and I want us to recognize that we don't have to be dependent on non-renewable energy. We can create a future of green technology and jobs. We can put a new premium on open spaces and our (suddenly) cleaner air and water. We can decide to learn from the glaring inequalities in our health system and focus on fixing them instead of denying or dismissing them as an unfortunate byproduct of modern society. Society doesn't have to look like the past—in fact, it can't. How can we re-envision a shared future with less inequality, with individual freedom tempered by collective liberty?

Eugene Ionesco said, "Ideologies separate us. Dreams and anguish bring us together." The pandemic gives us a chance to overcome ideologies and to dream big dreams, even as we work to relieve the immediate suffering of those in need.

Here's another thing I've noticed....

Other people in my house started getting up later and I've been getting up earlier, which has led me to dust off my meditation practice. There have been fits and starts and many times I just find myself staring at the beech tree, watching the changing light. One morning last week I was chewing my lip and staring at the beech tree when God sorta said in my head, *Hand me that worry and let me hold it awhile* and for some reason this didn't seem weird so I grudgingly let go of that one. 13 more popped up and God said, *Hand me 'self-image' to hold.* I was really resistant because I don't trust God to weigh or appreciate the bad parts enough and the self-image might come back changed, like God loving me as I am. But I handed it over. *Let me hold 'concern about children growing up to be fine adults' and, in fact, just hand over 'future' and you be here in *this* moment I've given you.*

I was still resisting, and God said, *You can have these things back if you want to pick them up again later.* God told me just to sit with my emotions—the sadness and grief and uncertainly—just to allow them. But I started wondering whether I could write about this and God said, *Stop. Just stop. Just be right here.* And I said, but I won't remember, and God said, *So?* And I said, but what if I forget what you want me to say? And God said, *If I want you to say it, you won't forget it.* And I said, promise? And God said, *Promise.* And I said, really really promise? And God said, *Stop it.*

Did I just lose you? Did you discount the voice in my head as, well, a voice in my head?

That's okay. I can't prove it; I can only tell you my truth. The voice isn't really a voice, and it both is and is not me. It is the part of me that observes myself. Have you ever said, "I can't stand myself today" or, better, "I'm proud of myself"? That observer is how I understand the soul, how the spark of divinity within each of God's creations shows itself in humans.

We cannot earn, invoke, incant, decant, conjure or become God. We can only accept and surrender to our original essence that is God; and then try to live out this Godliness as best we can. Recognizing and trusting this in me allows me to recognize and trust it in you. And in *Plestiodon fasciatus*, and these roses my friends brought to me, and that hawk that just landed outside my window.

I think it's what my friend, Bert, is saying here: "I go to Caw Caw swamp and meditate on the alligator hole in the freshwater marsh. Sometimes it's the limitless heaving and rippling grass that goes on to the horizon, sometimes it's the movement in the water of striped baby gators, sometimes it's just the whole inexpressible thing."

I've thought myself meditating when I was actually complaining and God has said, *what about that purple iris yesterday?* God keeps trying to break into my small world by speaking to me in my love language. People like to receive love the way they like to give love. Mark loves me by vacuuming. I give little gifts of noticing to the people I love. I show my family the secret home of the skinks. It's not really a secret, it's just that most folks don't notice. God does it for me, too, when I'm paying attention. God leaves little surprises for me to find: a frog here, a hawk there, buttery afternoon light on my laughing children, magnolia blossoms glowing against a storm-bruised sky. All these things hidden in plain view for me, for my delight. God bursting out of every leaf and amphibian for all to see. Any with eyes to see.

My children might prefer me to love them with candy and Legos instead of live skinks and dead turtles, but they'll have to settle for my noticing. The real gift is that there's always more to notice and understand. It's a daily practice that helps lessen my nostalgia for the future. I'm taking to heart Annie Dillard's observation that "How you spend your days is how you spend your life."

This pandemic is highlighting our society's flaws—our inequalities, our selfishness, our tendency to blame others. It is also highlighting the resilient human spirit—our desire to help, our willingness to sacrifice, our collective hope for the future. We all do what we can.

Knowing that you're doing your part gives me hope. I write to give you hope.

Hope in the whole inexpressible thing.

Afterword

Cave by Lis McLoughlin

The Enchantment of Nature and the Nature of Enchantment

Patrick Curry

My subject is double: the enchantment of nature, but also the nature of enchantment.[1] Enchantment is a fundamental human experience: the experience of wonder. So it is necessarily participatory, and therefore personal. Someone needs to actually be present for it. If you stay on the outside, merely observing, it can't happen. The word itself implies as much: from the French, originally Latin, *en chantment*: in a song. By extension, it might arise from finding yourself in a song that you are hearing or singing, or in a picture, or a story – in fact, any kind of narrative, in the very broadest sense.

The wonder varies in intensity from charm, to delight, to full-blown joy. We could also say 'awe'. (But note that I don't describe it as 'pleasure', which quality is somewhat different.) The last kind, joyful, is what I call 'radical enchantment'. It is normally something which only happens a few times in one's life, but it can be life-changing.

One clear opposite is will: any desire or effort to make something happen, to change something, or to make someone (including yourself) do something. If that is happening, then enchantment is not.

Enchantment is relational: wonder at another, not power over them. It takes place as an encounter, a meeting across a gap of difference. Those boundaries remain, but they no longer matter. So it's neither hot ecstatic unity, in which both self and other disappear, nor cold, one-way control over the other. And when enchantment is radical it is most relational, with each party apprehending and affecting the other.

Thus no one is in charge. Enchantment is wild and 'perilous'.[2] And this is something it shares with nature. In the whole more-than-human natural world,[3] including us but vastly greater, there are innumerable agents and very few outcomes are entirely predictable. This is why it arrives as a gift, or not at all.

Now the other party can be anyone or anything: a human being, another animal, plant, place of any kind, sight, sound, smell, taste, texture or even idea. But we are a particular kind of being – the human kind – and human nature is not, whatever our pretensions, infinitely plastic. So enchantment tends to happen with certain kinds of others and in certain domains: at a minimum, love, art, religion, food and drink, learning, sport, humour and, not least, nature: apprehending, in all its complexity, beauty and mystery, a natural place or fellow-creature, who sometimes, quite unexpectedly, apprehends you.

Actually, I believe all enchantments are ultimately natural, rooted in nature, including ourselves as natural beings. In other words, enchantment, like life, is not anthropocentric. It includes us but it isn't all about us, let alone me. (We shall return to this point.)

In the process of enchantment, the other becomes, and is realised to be, in effect, another person, with a unique personality of their own. Or, we could say, an extraordinary presence. Experiences of enchantment are thus intensely meaningful – and therefore fateful. (Even refusing them is fateful, because it always happens too late; you have already been affected.) Likewise, they are mythic. There are many modes of mythicity, some of them with nothing to do with wonder; but when you are enchanted, you are living mythically. In this respect too enchantment is rooted in nature. Ultimately, myths are not about the gods so much as 'the ideas and emotions of the Earth.'[4]

And what does enchantment show us about the enchanting other? It partly reveals, and partly creates, a truth: their intrinsic value and meaning, which doesn't depend in any way on their usefulness, or exchange value in the market.

Enchantment takes place as a unique moment – 'short but deep'[5] – so it doesn't happen in time – and as a unique place, so not in space. 'Nothing "happened", but everything has changed'.[6]

In the moment of enchantment, time radically slows. But it doesn't altogether stop, and sooner or later the enchantment comes to an end. So the wonder of childhood is continually becoming grown-up; wild nature is always falling to so-called development; and the Elves are forever passing over the Sea, leaving us behind on the darkening shores of Middle-earth in (god help us) 'the Age of Men', now known as the Anthropocene. Hence the joy of enchantment is often bittersweet, with a poignant or melancholy quality. By the same token, the quality of enchantment is not so much desire as it is yearning, or longing. The result can be a kind of pre-emptive nostalgia. In the words of the great haiku poet Bashō, 'Even in Kyōto, hearing the cuckoo cry, I long for Kyōto.'

Tolkien's name for the place of enchantment is Faërie, and he describes it as 'the realm or state in which fairies have their being. [But] Faërie contains many things besides elves and fays...it holds the seas, the sun, the moon, the sky; and the earth, and all things that are in it: tree and bird, water and stone, wine and bread, and ourselves...when we are enchanted.'[7] So Faërie is the place you find yourself in when you are enchanted, and it is what the place where you are becomes.

The difference between infinite and very, very large is important, because the latter finally has its limits. And just as enchanted moments do not last forever, however much they feel that way at the time, we cannot stay forever in Faërie, only visit or be visited by it. (We are humans, not Elves.) It follows that a healthy relationship with enchantment needs a strong ego, to let go when needs must, and not fall into futile grasping or clinging.

Enchantment as 'concrete magic': both utterly particular – this person, in this precise moment and place – and inexhaustible, mysterious.[8] In other words, it is both embodied, even carnal, and spiritual. By the same token, enchantment is neither purely 'subjective' nor purely 'objective'. It is upstream of that distinction.

The spiritual dimension of enchantment – its 'magic' – is therefore not something floating above concrete circumstances, or added to it, as the word 'supernatural' implies. It only exists in, and as, those circumstances: not the contrary of the world of the senses but 'its lining and its depth'; in short, its meaning.[9] And the farther in you go, the more 'transcendental' it becomes.

Out of many candidates, let me give three instances of natural enchantment. One I'm fond of is a report dated March 23, 1926 by a Mr E.O. Grant, and you should factor in the ultra-laconic verbal style of New England rural folk:

> Saw farmer near Patten, Maine, sitting on a snowdrift about fifteen feet high, surrounded by a hundred redpolls. Birds perched on the farmer's head and shoulders. One sat on knee. Farmer told Grant that he had enjoyed the previous half hour more than any other period in his life.[10]

Going deeper – but not necessarily more moving – is another account by the writer Richard Mabey, describing listening to a nightingale sing in a Suffolk fen, under a full moon, one early May night:

> He sings a stylish four-note phrase, then repeats it in a minor key. He slides into a bubbling tremolo on a single note and holds it for more than ten seconds. How does he breathe? I can't believe he is not consciously improvising. I want to clap and with barely credible timing, a shooting star arcs over the bush in which he is singing.
>
> I'm edging closer now without realising it and am now no more than ten feet away. Nothing stops the flow of notes. They fill the air, they seem to be solid, to be doing odd things to the light. I am half-aware that my peripheral vision is closing down, and that I am riveted to the bush by this tunnel of intense sound.

At that point, 'just for a few seconds, the bird was in my head and it was me that was singing.' Then, remembering Shelley's lines describing the effect of nightingale song as 'So sweet, that joy is almost pain', Mabey questions his own response. He concludes that it is different, but 'the effort breaks the spell', and he walks regretfully away.[11]

This is a classic instance of enchantment. It includes sheer presence – participation – the relationality of wonder-at – embodied, especially as the sense of hearing, and embedded in a very particular place – the concrete magic of the bird's singing, at once 'material' and 'spiritual' – and an aspect of enchantment I haven't been able to explore here, namely the 'tensive truth' of living metaphor.[12] Mabey is both himself, a human, and a nightingale; and he is both singing and not singing.

Finally, a story of my own which I bring forward because it shows how natural enchantment goes even further in challenging the modernist prejudice which confines subjectivity and agency to 'inside' human heads (as if the mind, unlike the brain, had an 'inside' or 'outside'!), sometimes grudgingly extended to a few 'higher' animals. Because this time – as often happens – the enchanting other is not a biological entity, strictly speaking, but a place.

In his classic wondertale of 1871, George MacDonald says that in the country at the back of the North Wind, there is a river that 'flows not through but over grass: its channel, instead of being rock, stones, pebbles, sand, or anything else, was of pure meadow grass, not overlong.' In 2004, a friend took me for a walk in Nakajimadai Recreation Park in Shishigahana Shitsugen, at the foot of Mount Chokai in Akita Prefecture, Japan. And there, in a forest at the foot of the mountain, although not looking for it, I found it. I had never been for a walk with a river before. Not by, but with. It flowed freely where it would, not taking a predetermined or even self-created course in a riverbed but among grass, moss and dead leaves, through the forest. And we walked alongside it, the three of us keeping each other company. (The glowing blues and greens were so intense that most people, seeing the photographs, assume they had been Photoshopped… What an imagination my camera must have!)

Let's return to my earlier claim that all enchantments are natural. They are wonder at, or enchantment by, and therefore relational – which is to say, ecological, in the broadest and deepest sense. They take place in nature as experiences of concrete magic, in which the carnal embodiment of the enchanted is actively present, as is that of the enchanting one, in whatever form. And ultimately they occur as nature: instances or incarnations of the more-than-human world, which includes us as natural beings. (It is also quite capacious enough to include spirits, gods or goddesses. Even, I daresay, cyborgs.) In short, enchantment is an inalienable part of life; its potential is inherent in being alive as embodied, ecological, interdependent, finite Earthlings. But it is also wonder at being alive! An astonishing and humbling apprehension of 'wild Being',[13] incarnated as this particular precious, vulnerable other being, triumphantly themself, before another one, affirmed in your affirmation of them: you.

Despite its apparent fluffiness, then, enchantment has profound pragmatic consequences, not least respecting our relationship with the natural world. Because in the end, we will only fight to defend what we have been enchanted by and learned to value and love. Reason alone, although important, isn't enough when it stands alone. This point finds a special resonance in the most serious crisis of all that is facing us: not COVID-19, but the ecocide of which it is only one result. Again, good policy and science are needed, but without personal wonder in and at the natural world, they are ultimately blind. It is enchantment that opens our eyes.

ENDNOTES

1 For a longer and deeper treatment, see my *Enchantment: Wonder in Modern Life* (Edinburgh: Floris Books, 2019).

2 Verlyn Flieger and Douglas A. Anderson (eds), *Tolkien on Fairy-stories, expanded edition, with commentary and notes* (London: HarperCollins, 2008): passim.

3 David Abram, *The Spell of the Sensuous: Perception and Language in a More-Than-Human World* (New York: Vintage Books, 1996).

4 Sean Kane, *Wisdom of the Mythtellers, rev. edn* (Peterborough: Broadview Press, 1998): 34.

5 Etel Adnan, from a notice in an exhibition of her work in Basle, 2017.

6 Eduardo Viveiros de Castro, MS., 'Cosmological Perspectivism in Amazonia and Elsewhere', four lectures given at the University of Cambridge in 1998: 63.

7 Flieger and Anderson, *Tolkien*: 32.

8 H.H. Gerth and C. Wright Mills (eds.), *From Max Weber: Essays in Sociology* (London: Routledge, 1991): 282.

9 Maurice Merleau-Ponty, *The Visible and the Invisible*, ed. Claude Lefort and transl. Alphonso Lingis (Evanston: Northwestern University Press, 1968): 149.

10 *Essays of E.B. White* (New York: Harper & Row, 1977): 274.

11 Richard Mabey, *The Barley Bird. Notes on the Suffolk Nightingale* (Woodbridge: Full Circle

Editions, 2010) 17-18; cf. his *The Book of Nightingales* (London: Sinclair_Stevenson, 1997): 8-9.

12 See Paul Ricoeur, *The Rule of Metaphor. The Creation of Meaning in Language*, transl. Robert Czerny (London: Routledge, 2003)

13 *Merleau-Ponty, Visible:* passim.

Postscript

It is my cultural and spiritual experience that Earth is our Mother. It is from her and Great Spirit that I /we all evolve. Every you, every me, every tree, every blade of grass, pebble, and stone, and every worm between---every bee and bird, every fish, every grape, and apple--- every mosquito, and fly--has our Mother as our source. With her, things remain in harmony and balance. We are of her natural world. We are earthlings and natural order manifested by the coming together of Great Spirit and the being we know as Earth. From her we come and back to her we return---we the dolphin, the whale, the clam, the ameba, the virus---all of us. Whether Alewife or Buckeye or *Nenhaden* she has instructed us if we plant them in the Earth below the corn it fertilizes and a hill of corn shall grow. We are dependent and she is wise in the way of sustaining her children. She is mother and we are her earthlings. We are sometimes obedient, sometimes arrogant, but her children nonetheless.

Tau batdan-tamock wtche wane (we are giving thanks for all things).
-- Doug Harris, Preservationist for Ceremonial Landscapes

~

Doug Harris- In 1663 Qunimequin (Longfeather), my paternal ancestor departed from his Sockanossett-Narragansett village in colonial Rhode Island as a mate on a maritime schooner headed for the riverine communities of the Chesapeake Bay of Virginia. He disembarked there and adopted the name Josephus Harris. The Harris name was known to him from Rhode Island. From the riverine Tribal communities of the Chesapeake his Harris descendants migrated to the North Carolina foothills of the Blue Ridge Mountains. His Harris descendants intermarried with the descendants of Tuscarora Chief Billy Mitchell making me a seventh grandson of the Carolina Tuscarora chief. In 1963 I responded to Dr. Martin Luther King's call for students to assist with voter liberation in the deep south. In ceremony with my maternal Saponi/Cherokee grandfather I was admonished that if I was to serve in the land of cotton I must be there on behalf of my Cheraw grandmother's ancestors and their Choctaw and Southern Cherokee ancestors who required freedom from the effects of colonial slavery. He stated that if you are to risk your life, do so for the lands of your ancestors. For the next four years I served with others to bring empowerment of the right to vote to the lands of the Cheraw, Choctaw, and Southern Cherokee.

In time I was to marry the eldest daughter of the Narragansett medicine woman Ella Sekatau who is now herself the Tribe's medicine woman. The ceremonial guidance I sought in Narragansett country led me to my work as Preservationist for Ceremonial Landscapes.

~

Authors' Biographies

Dr. Gay Bradshaw holds doctorate degrees in ecology and psychology, a master's in geophysics, and a bachelors in linguistics and Chinese. She is the founder and director of The Kerulos Center for Nonviolence and The Tortoise and the Hare Sanctuary located in Jacksonville, Oregon, USA.

Martin Bridge's work spans a wide range of media from Drawing, Painting, Sculpture, Theater Design and Site Specific Installations to Performance. He bridges realms of science and mysticism in an effort to challenge the cultural paradigms that dictate how we relate to both the natural world as well as our brothers and sisters.
https://www.thebridgebrothers.com www.patreon.com/martinclarkbridge

Rebecca R Burrill, EdD is a movement-based child developmentalist and educator, ecocentric dancer, artistic director, and writer. She is founder of an alternative educational organization providing programing such as Arts with Literacy Integration™
http://horsechestnutwinds.com/

Susan Cerulean is an author and a naturalist. Her most recent book, *I Have Been Assigned the Single Bird: A Daughter's Memoir*, was published in August 2020. With her husband Jeff Chanton, she divides her time between Indian Pass and Tallahassee, Florida.

David Crews (he/him) is author of two poetry collections that catalog his hiking of the "Adirondack 46ers" (8385) in upstate New York. Crews serves as resident artist with ARTS By The People, as well as a contributing writer for the Northeast Wilderness Trust.
www.davidcrewspoetry.com

Candace Curran is a founding member of multimedia exhibitions throughout Western MA. Twice named Poet's Seat Laureate, publications include, *Bone Cages* and *Playing in Wrecks* and journals, Raw NerVZ , Meat for Tea among others. A Straw Dog member from Franklin County, she lives Buckland side of the Iron Bridge in Shelburne Falls.

Patrick Curry is a Canadian-born writer and scholar living in England. He holds a PhD in the History and Philosophy of Science and is a Tutor at the University of Wales. He is the author of *Enchantment* (2019) among other books and the Editor-in-Chief of *The Ecological Citizen* (http://www.ecologicalcitizen.net), as well as a *Companion of the Guild of St George*. www.patrickcurry.co.uk

Carlos Raúl Dufflar is celebrating 26 years as Founder and Artistic Director of The Bread is Rising Poetry Collective. He is also the New York City Beat Poet Laureate for 2020-2022. http://www.thebreadisrising.org/

Marty Espinola became interested in photography at the age of 15. Later as a school teacher he worked weekends as a newspaper and freelance photographer. Now retired, he enjoys pursuing his love of nature photography, mentoring local photography groups and doing workshops. https://lighteffects.shutterfly.com.

Susan Glass's poetry appeared most recently in *Fire and Rain: Ecopoetry of California*. Her forthcoming chapbook, *The Wild Language of Deer*, will be released by Slate Roof Press in 2021. She lives in Saratoga California with her husband John, and her yellow Labrador Retriever guide dog Omni.

Jason Grundstrom-Whitney, a Bear Clan member of the Passamaquoddy Tribe, is a musician who plays various wind instruments for classical, jazz, rock, funk, country, blues, and rap. The band Osha Root recently produced a CD featuring Jason's music and poetry. His poetry has appeared in *3 Nations Anthology: Native, Canadian & New England Writers* and in the *Underground Writers Association's Anthology of Maine Poets*.

Dr. Deb Habib is a co-founder with Ricky Baruch of the solar-powered, no-till, regenerative Seeds of Solidarity Farm and Education Center in Orange MA. Their non-profit wing innovates Grow Food Everywhere, and they co-organize the North Quabbin Garlic and Arts Festival. Ricky and Deb are authors of *Making Love While Farming: A Field Guide to a Life of Passion and Purpose*.

Holly Harden At age nine, on the way home from a funeral, she began to write, and she's been writing ever since. Holly's nonfiction has appeared in *Utne* and *Fourth Genre*, and she edited Garrison Keillor's *Good Poems and Life Among the Lutherans*. Her books include *Good Food from Mrs. Sundberg's Kitchen*, and *Recipes for Gatherings from Mrs. Sundberg's Kitchen*.

Richard Wayne Horton creates prose poetry, flash fiction and longer fiction. He likes to mix genres. He has received 2 Pushcart nominations and is the 2019-21 Massachusetts Beat Poet Laureate. His books include *Sticks & Bones*, and *Artists In The Underworld*. He has published in *Lonesome October, Meat For Tea, Bull & Cross, Literary Heist, The Dead Mule* and others. albumsandsuch@ gmail.com.

Dr. Leo L. Hwang is the Assistant Academic Dean in the College of Natural Sciences Academic Advising Center at the University of Massachusetts, Amherst. He earned his Ph.D. in Geosciences, his M.F.A. in fiction writing, and his B.A. in English and Fine Arts. His work has appeared in numerous academic and literary publications.

JuPong Lin is an interdisciplinary artist originally from Taiwan, based in the traditional homelands of the Pocumtuck. As an artist, de/colonial and institutional activist and educator, she makes art to bridge personal and collective healing, and to revitalize our lands and skies from the ravages of colonialism and extractive capitalism. JuPong currently chairs the MFA in Interdisciplinary Arts program at Goddard College.

Janet MacFadyen managing editor of Slate Roof Press, has a poetry collection forthcoming from Salmon Poetry. She authored 5 books including *Adrift in the House of Rocks, Waiting to Be Born*, and *In the Provincelands*. Recent works in *Scientific American, Naugatuck River Review, CALYX, Sweet, The Blue Nib, Tiny Seed Journal, Q/A Poetry,* and *Terrain*.

Joan Maloof is an ecologist and conservationist whose formal education includes a bachelor's in Plant Science, a master's in Environmental Science, and a Doctorate in Ecology. She is professor emeritus at Salisbury University and author of numerous research articles and five books including the forthcoming *Treepedia* (2021). Maloof founded the Old-Growth Forest Network with the goal of creating a network of protected forests across the US. www.JoanMaloof.com

Ángel L. Martínez is on the road of Year 26 of The Bread is Rising Collective as Deputy Artistic Director. Can you believe it? More to the point, can you feel what that means to share words after so long?

Christian McEwen is a freelance writer, workshop leader, and cultural activist, originally from the UK. Her book, *World Enough & Time: On Creativity* and *Slowing Down* (2011) is now in its seventh printing. She is currently working on a manuscript called *In Praise of Listening*. www.christianmcewen.com

Lis McLoughlin holds a BS in Civil Engineering, and a PhD in Science and Technology Studies. Her published works include academic articles, poems, personal essays, a stage performance, book chapters, and newspaper articles. Her current work is focused on how writing and activism connect people to the rest of Nature. https://nature-culture.net

Don Ogden (d.o.) has been active in environmental issues for most of his life. His poetry and commentaries have appeared in a wide variety of publications, in ecologically-themed street theater, and on local and national radio. His book, *Bad Atmosphere – A Collection of Poetry & Prose on the Climate Crisis* contains decades of writing on climate issues http://concertobi.blogspot.com/

Robert Eugene Perry is a metaphysical poet native to Massachusetts. His first novel *Where the Journey Takes You*, was published in 2007, followed by three collections of poetry. Two of Perry's poems were published in Poetica Magazine's 2020 *Mizmor anthology*. His poem "Quest" was the January 2019 Poets of Mars winner. roberteugeneperry@myportfolio.com

Paul Rabinowitz is an author, photographer and founder of ARTS By The People. Paul's photography, short fiction and poetry have appeared in many magazines and journals and he is the author of 2 books. Paul has produced mixed media performances and poetry animation films that have appeared on stages and in theaters from New York, to Tel Aviv, to Paris. www.paulrabinowitz.com

Kate Rex poet/translator /feminist/artist/subversive/political activist, always vigilant and deeply critical. She is European and lives principally in the clear light of the south of France, at other times in Glasgow, Scotland. She writes in English and in French. Her writing makes the links. She says it's the process that unearths the connections and the juxtapositions that make the spaces, just like painting really.

Paul Richmond was named Beat Poet Laureate twice, MA 2017 to 2019, and then U S National Beat Poet Laureate 2019- 2020. He has performed nationally and internationally as a featured poet. He has 6 books published. www.humanerrorpublishing.com

Cheryl Savageau is the author of the memoir, *Out of the Crazywoods*, and of the poetry collections, *Dirt Road Home*, which was nominated for a Pulitzer Prize, and *Mother/Land*. Her children's book, *Muskrat Will Be Swimming* won the Skipping Stones Book Award for Exceptional Multicultural and Ecology and Nature Books. She teaches at the Bread Loaf School of English at Middlebury College.

Julia Sibley-Jones lives in Greenville, South Carolina, with her husband and their two children. She is the Director of Development for Upstate Fatherhood Coalition. She likes to ask her children when they noticed God today. Their answers are often much better than hers. www.ThisUnchartedNow.org

Cindy Snow's writing has appeared in the *Massachusetts Review*, *Peace Review*, *Worcester Review*, *Crannóg*, and elsewhere, and her chapbook, *Small Ceremonies*, was published by Slate Roof Press. Her poetry has been nominated for a Pushcart and has won a variety of prizes. Cindy holds an MFA in Poetry from Drew University, and she works at Greenfield Community College, Greenfield, MA.

Janice Sorensen has received grants in art and writing and is a published poet and art critic. She is the founding member of Cloud Saddle Writers and a member of Straw Dog Writers. Currently, an artist and interior designer, she lives with her partner, Michael and a fluctuating number of critters at Magpie Farm & Art, in Buckland, Massachusetts.

Zarnab Tufail is currently an upcoming medical student in Pakistan and on staff at *Variety Pack*, *Tiny Molecules*, and *The Lumiere Review*. She experiments with poetry, photography, painting, and journaling. She is the co-founder of *The Walled City Journal*, and her work has been published in or is forthcoming in at least 6 publications. www.zarnabtufail.wordpress.com

Karen Warinsky's work has been published by the Montreal International Poetry Contest, the anthology *Nuclear Impact: Broken Atoms in Our Hands*, and several lit journals. Her first collection of verse, *Gold in Autumn*, was released in 2020. She organizes poetry readings in Connecticut and Massachusetts. Reach her on Twitter @KWarinsky, or karen.warinsky@gmail.com.

Anna M. Warrock's *From the Other Room* won the Slate Roof Press Chapbook Award. Besides appearing in *The Sun, The Madison Review, Harvard Review,* and other journals, her work is anthologized in *Kiss Me Goodnight*, women writing on childhood mother-loss, a Minnesota Book Award Finalist. Her poems have been choreographed and inscribed in a Boston area subway station. www.AnnaMWarrock.com

Lise Weil is editor of *Dark Matter: Women Witnessing*, a journal devoted to healing our broken relationship to the earth. Her memoir *In Search of Pure Lust* was a finalist for an International Book Award. She teaches in Goddard College's Graduate Institute, where she helped found a concentration in Embodiment Studies. www.liseweil.com

Roger West Faithful to the letter / an avowed user of vowels / with a constancy of consonants / a capital character up to the mark / soni- cally phonic / hieroglyphically prolific / enigmatically monogrammatic / an assembler of emblems / a rifler through cyphers / attuned to the rune / well cunieformed / and minusculed in the rigours of figures. The rest is just words. www.rogerwestmusic.com

Dr. Simon Wilson is a Senior Lecturer in the Faculty of Arts, Humanities and Education at Canterbury Christ Church University in the UK, and a member of the Institute for Orthodox Christian Studies at Cambridge, UK. He has a special interest in landscape, co-creation, love of learning, spirituality, and the true nature of sustainability, and has published in 3 anthologies, and edited another.

David Wyman's poetry collections *Violet Ideologies* (2020) and *Proletariat Sunrise* (2017) were published by Kelsay Books. His poems have appeared in *BlazeVOX, Dissident Voice, Zombie Logic Review, Clockwise Cat, Tuck Magazine* among other publications

Credit for Previous Publication
(page #s below refer to this volume)

Burrill, Rebecca R - This article is partially excerpted from "Dancing our Kinship with Animate Earth" in *Minding Nature*, Vol. 9. No. 1 (January 2016), a publication of the Center for Humans and Nature (www.humansandnature.org) page 113

Crews, David - after Cathy Hartung's painting (NorthWind Fine Arts, Saranac Lake, NY, April 2020) page 57

Grundstrom-Whitney, Jason - both poems first published by Resolute Bear Press   page 70   page 97

Maloof, Joan - Excerpted from *TREEPEDIA: A Brief Compendium of Arboreal Lore* by Joan Maloof. Copyright © 2021 by Joan Maloof. Reprinted by permission of Princeton University Press page 119

McEwen, Christian - excerpted from *In Praise of Listening*, forthcoming page 121

d. o. - 2020 Highlights was published in an earlier form in The *Amherst Bulletin* and performed on Dave Rovics' 'Pandemic Open Mic Monday' on Youtube, both in 2020 page 84

Savageau, Cheryl - "Red" first appeared in *Gatherings*, Fall 1998, and is in *Mother/Land*, Salt Publishing, 2006 page 21; "Swift River" from *Mother/Land*, page 33; "What It Is For" was published in a different form in *Three Nations Anthology*, Resolute Bear Press, and in *Mother/Land* page 132

Warinsky, Karen - published in the anthology, *Nuclear Impact: Broken Atoms in our Hands*, Shabda Press, 2017   page 81

Warrock, Anna M. - "The Salmon Go All the Way Upstream" is from her chapbook *From the Other Room*, Slate Roof Press, published in 2017 page 35

Weil, Lise - excerpted from *Feminist Pilgrimage: Journeys of Discovery* editor Stacy Russo page 102

Artists' Credits

cover: Photosynthesis by Martin Bridge
https://www.thebridgebrothers.com

Great White Egret Fishing by Marty Espinola
https://lighteffects.shutterfly.com   page 11

Embracing the Light by Vic Berardi   page 19

Enders Falls by Marty Espinola https://lighteffects.shutterfly.com page 29

Desert View Watchtower by Cate Woolner
https://www.facebook.com/Woolnerphotos   page 37

Canoe Catch by JuPong Lin https://www.juponglin.net   page 43

Untitled by Fred Bulye https://nektos.net   page 55

Prophecy Infection by ARTMUFFIN www.artmuffin.com
Instagram: artmuffin_studio   page 69

The Red Rebel Brigade by Cate Woolner
https://www.facebook.com/Woolnerphotos   page 91

Lis on the Rocks by Helene D. Grogan
http://www.helenegrogan.com   page 101

Callanish I by Lis McLoughlin
http://nature-culture.net   page 131

Cave by Lis McLoughlin http://nature-culture.net   page 141

Acknowledgements

I am grateful to all the lithic beings who inspire, direct, and assist my work, with special thanks to the stones of Northfield, Massachusetts; Salem, Massachusetts; Cayman Brac; the Isle of Lewis and Harris; and Montreal. To my grandfather, a builder of ships, thank you for encouraging me to explore the stones on the shore and under the sea; and to Doug Harris, thank you for teaching me how to be in service to them. -L.M.

Human Error PUBLISHING is an independent publishing house and is very excited about adding this manuscript to its aritists' roster. HEP is looking forward to working with NatureCulture on projects like this, related to land and the sacredness of the land. Protecting this environment which makes it possible for us to experience this beautiful world seems obvious, I wish it was.

Human Error Publishing is dedicated to developing and showcasing artists of all types and is involved in organizing and producing annual and monthly WORD Festivals & Events. These events are curated performances which take place either online or in brick and mortar venues when possible, post - Covid 19 virus. Human Error Publishing is also a co-host on a weekly radio show. Human Error Publishing is owned and operated by Paul Richmond
https://www.humanerrorpublishing.com/